ROCK SOLID

ROCK SOLID

My Life in Baseball's Fast Lane

Tim Raines with Alan Maimon

TRIUMPH
BOOKS

Library of Congress Cataloging-in-Publication Data available upon request

This book is available in quantity at special discounts for your group or organization. For further information, contact:

Triumph Books LLC
814 North Franklin Street
Chicago, Illinois 60610
(312) 337-0747
www.triumphbooks.com

Printed in U.S.A.
ISBN: 978-1-62937-400-0
Design by Patricia Frey

To my parents, Ned and Florence

Contents

Foreword

THE FIRST TIME I SAW Tim Raines in action was at the end of the 1979 season, when he got called up to Montreal from the minor leagues. My first impression of him was that he didn't look like most baseball players I knew. Built like a running back, he was short and squat (solid as a rock, you might say), and his lightning-fast sprints during pregame warmups only added to his football player vibe. He also had a real baby face, but that shouldn't have been surprising considering he was just a 19-year-old kid.

Some friendships develop quickly. Two people meet, hit it off right away, and remain close from that point on. Well, that isn't how it played out for Rock and me. In fact, there was a real awkwardness to our first interactions with each other. During one of our early conversations, he told me about the time in high school that he went to an Expos spring training game in Orlando and asked me for an autograph, a request I flatly denied. I told him I had no recollection of the encounter, and to be honest, I couldn't imagine that I would act rudely toward an autograph seeker. My Expos teammates knew me as a reserved person who didn't smile a whole lot. The new kid on the block apparently hadn't received that memo. My stone-faced reaction to what he intended as a funny story probably didn't help make him feel any less nervous about being around major-leaguers in general and me in particular.

It took a while for Rock to settle into his career. Everyone could see that he ran like the wind, but he really struggled at the plate during his early days in the majors. The raw ability was there. He just needed to build up his confidence and find a way to harness his talent. And that's exactly what he did in 1981. The kid who showed up to camp in '81 had a totally different aura than the one who left to play winter ball in the Dominican Republic a few months earlier. In his rookie season, Rock was an unstoppable force, knocking the ball all over the park and stealing bases almost at will. We both had great seasons, among the best of our respective careers, despite losing a large chunk of games to a two-month strike. And the Expos made it all the way to the National League Championship Series, where we lost in heartbreaking fashion to the Dodgers.

I got to know Rock the player very well during his rookie season, but I couldn't say that I knew Rock the person quite yet. As the team's Florida-born starting outfield trio, he, Warren Cromartie, and I spent a lot of time together at the ballpark, but our conversations tended to center on baseball and never got too deep. Our non-sports-related talks usually consisted of restaurant recommendations or sharing information about hurricanes that were hitting back home. There wasn't much hanging out. After games, we went our separate ways.

Adversity brought Rock and me together. I'm not the type of person to tell someone else how to run his life, so when I started hearing rumblings about Rock's personal problems during the 1982 season, I decided it wasn't my place to intervene. After the story of his battle with cocaine hit the papers, however, I realized I needed to get involved. I saw Rock's potential as a ballplayer, teammate, and friend, and hated the thought that he might travel any further down the road to disaster. If keeping the wrong company had helped contribute to his situation, then I vowed to make sure that he started keeping the right company.

"Come on, homey," I told him. "That's not you. That's not what you're about. I'm going to keep you close to me from now on."

It didn't take much convincing on my part to get Rock to agree to that plan. He decided on his own that it was what he needed to do.

Our friendship went to a new level. We talked, actually *talked*. I told him about things in my life that weren't perfect and he opened up to me about the struggles in his life. But mostly we just hung out and enjoyed each other's company. He and his wife at the time, Virginia, became regulars at our apartment. Virginia and my wife, Vanessa, also struck up a friendship. When Rock and Virginia's second son was born in 1983—on my birthday, of all days—they named him after me and asked that I be his godfather. I felt incredibly honored.

It was so much fun to be around Rock. He used to show me film of him playing football in high school. I laughed at how wide his eyes got as we watched the old footage. As a former high school football player myself, I had to admit that he had been a talented running back. If he found a hole and broke through the line, there wasn't much chance of catching him. That speed set him up nicely for a major league career. But he didn't want just to be known as a guy who stole a lot of bases. I admire how hard he worked to become a complete player. He always carried around a book titled *The Art of Hitting .300*. In the book, legendary hitting instructor Charlie Lau instructs players to stand in front of a mirror and take imaginary swings. So that's what Rock constantly did in the clubhouse, much to the amusement of all of his teammates. It worked, though.

Thanks to Rock, I started having more fun at the ballpark. Sometimes he was like a pesky gnat that would fly up and buzz in your ear until you swatted it away. He did things to me that no one else in the Expos clubhouse would have dreamed of doing, including coming up from behind me and delivering a couple of quick jabs to my back before running off. My instinct was to give chase, but I realized I wouldn't be able to catch him. Rock wasn't a clown, but he definitely had a real comedian in him. While I became known for my serious and focused approach to the game, Rock wore the joy of baseball (and life) on his sleeve. His carefree personality helped loosen me up. There were many times when I'd be sitting in the Expos clubhouse, locked inside myself, not saying much, and Rock would come along and rib me until I relaxed.

I think Rock and I both would have been happy to stay in Montreal for our entire careers. But that's not how it worked out. I'll never forget our time together with the Expos. Who knows, maybe a major league team will return to Montreal someday. If that ever happens, Rock and I will be its biggest cheerleaders. After we both became victims of collusion, I went to the Cubs in 1987, while Rock remained with the Expos for a few more seasons. As it turned out, we both ended up in Chicago in the early 1990s.

We didn't get much of an opportunity to see each other during his time with the White Sox, but he was always around if I needed him, and vice versa.

As my knee problems worsened and eventually led me to hang it up, Rock just kept chugging along. In 1996, he got to experience something I never did when he won a World Series title. The morning after his Yankees team clinched it, I called him up to ask what it felt like to be a champion. He told me about the wild celebration the night before and talked about how fortunate he was to be in the right place at the right time that season. I retired never having played in a World Series, the biggest regret of my career, but it made me feel better to know that my best friend in baseball was experiencing so much joy.

I can't tell you how happy I am that Rock and I overcame our initial wariness of each other. On the field, we helped the Expos win a lot of games in the 1980s, and off the field we developed a friendship based on mutual respect that has stood the test of time. Rock likes to say that I had a big impact on his life and career. Well, I can definitely say the same thing about him. Rock's impact on me was huge, and I'm a better person for knowing him.

We've remained close over the years. Whenever we get together, we laugh and rehash old times. Every January for the past several years, I've called him up on the day of the announcement of the new Hall of Fame class. Usually, the purpose of the call was to keep his spirits up by letting him know that he deserved a spot in the Hall and just needed to remain patient. Your time will come, I told him, reminding him that it took me nine years to get the call to Cooperstown.

When I saw Rock at an event in the summer of 2016, I told him not to expect a call from me the following January. "I won't need to cheer you up this time around," I said. So I congratulated him then and there and told him I'd see him in Cooperstown in July 2017. I wouldn't miss it for the world.

Andre Dawson played 21 seasons in the major leagues with the Montreal Expos, Chicago Cubs, Boston Red Sox, and Florida Marlins. He was the National League Rookie of the Year in 1977, the NL MVP in 1987, and was inducted into the National Baseball Hall of Fame in 2010.

Introduction

I SPENT A GOOD CHUNK of the past decade advocating for Tim Raines to get into the Hall of Fame. The day his name was announced as a 2017 inductee was one of the most gratifying days of my life.

First, I was happy to see Raines' on-field accomplishments finally, fully recognized.

For many years, the gold standard for Hall of Fame induction was 3,000 hits. What made Raines so great as a leadoff man, though, was his ability to get on base through any means necessary. While he fell a bit short of the magic number, with 2,605 hits, he also walked 1,330 times in his career. Put it all together, and Raines reached base more times than Hall of Famers Tony Gwynn, Lou Brock, Roberto Clemente, Mike Schmidt, Roberto Alomar, Eddie Mathews, Brooks Robinson, and Harmon Killebrew.

Once he reached base, Rock terrorized opposing pitchers. Only five players in baseball history have ever stolen 800 bases: Rickey Henderson, Ty Cobb, Lou Brock, 19th century star Billy Hamilton…and Raines. Stealing bases only helps your team if you can do so without getting caught often. No problem there:

of all the players in baseball history with 400 or more attempts, the most efficient base stealer of all time is...Raines, who swiped successfully 84.7 percent of the time.

Venturing into the world of advanced stats only strengthened Raines' case further. Wins Above Replacement is a metric that measures everything a player does—not just hits, walks, and home runs, but also defense and base running, all while adjusting for factors such as league quality and how a player's home ballpark affects offense. During the best five-year stretch of Raines' career, from 1983 through 1987, the best player in the National League by Wins Above Replacement was...Raines. Don't want to cherry-pick that peak period? No problem. From 1981 through 1990, the best player in the National League by Wins Above Replacement wasn't Andre Dawson, Dale Murphy, Mike Schmidt, Ozzie Smith, Gary Carter, or Keith Hernandez. It was Raines.

Impartial numbers don't even begin to tell the story, though.

Growing up in Montreal as a kid in the 1980s, I rarely thought about Raines' on-base percentage, and certainly never thought about any fancier stats than that. We would venture out to Olympic Stadium, settle in for the bottom of the first, and bear witness to the most electrifying player in the league. Every time Raines got on base, a buzz would crackle through the building, every fan perched on the edge of his seat, waiting for lightning to strike. Everyone in the ballpark knew what was going to happen.

Rock wasn't merely the most exciting player in the National League. He was the most fun to watch. Every time a pitcher threw over to first base, the old scoreboard at the Big O would light up with...chickens. Low-tech, cartoon chickens, designed to mock opponents into throwing the damn pitch, so that Raines could finally take off. Rock loved the chickens. He'd make it his mission to set personal chicken records—seven, eight, nine, 10 throws over—as he drove pitchers to distraction. Imagine those being your formative experiences as a baseball fan, going to the ballgame with your grandfather and watching your favorite player conjure nine innings' worth of clucking. Raines should've been inducted into the Hall of Fame solely for reigning for a decade as the undisputed King of Chickens.

As great a player as Raines was, as fun to watch as he was, all of that pales compared to the kind of man he is.

When a teammate got down, Raines was Mr. Sunshine, cracking jokes and lifting spirits.

When a cocaine addiction threatened to ruin his career and his life, Raines took responsibility. He told all to the media, sought help and guidance from his friend and mentor Andre Dawson, and got clean.

When Derek Jeter and a new generation of Yankees needed a veteran leader who could get on base and inspire the kids with a loose brand of baseball, they called on Raines. In his first season in pinstripes, the Bombers won it all, starting a new dynasty in the Bronx.

Very few of us ever get to meet our heroes. If and when the opportunity does arise, what's the best you can hope for? A semi-polite hello? A perfunctory, five-second interaction?

Meeting and then getting to know Raines has offered so much more. The man I once knew only as a darting figure on the base paths has proven to be unfailingly kind.

And funny. Oh man, is this guy funny. One summer night in Kansas City, I was hosting an event, with Raines and Dawson scheduled to join me on stage. Time was ticking and I was getting a little nervous. So I called Rock.

"Hey, are you almost here?" I asked, slightly panicked.

"Our flight got delayed. It'll be at least two hours."

(Long, panicked silence)

"Just kidding, man! See you in a minute."

From a face on a baseball card to a father of twins who asks a fellow dad with twins for life advice, Raines has evolved from the object of my early fandom to a generous (and hilarious) friend.

Hall of Fame ballplayer. Hall of Fame human being. Mazel tov, Rock.

Jonah Keri is the author of the New York Times *best sellers* The Extra 2% *and* Up, Up, & Away. *He writes about baseball for CBS Sports and* Sports Illustrated. *He has also covered baseball and other sports for* Grantland, ESPN, The New York Times, *the* Wall Street Journal, Baseball Prospectus, Bloomberg Sports, FanGraphs, *and many other publications. Follow him on Twitter @JonahKeri.*

CHAPTER ONE

1

IT'S INCREDIBLE WHAT A DIFFERENCE two days can make.

On June 27, 1982, I stood on top of the world, fresh off the type of game that had solidified my reputation as one of the fastest-rising stars in the major leagues. In a Sunday afternoon win against the Pittsburgh Pirates that brought my Montreal Expos within a game of first place, I went 3-for-3 with two walks and three stolen bases.

Not a bad performance considering I had been up all night partying on Crescent Street in downtown Montreal.

With a day off before our next series at Olympic Stadium, I decided to keep the good times rolling. I hit up the locales where I knew I could score cocaine, which had become my drug of choice earlier that season. The next 48 hours were a blur. As I crisscrossed Montreal, snorting line after line, my mind started playing tricks on me. I saw objects and heard voices that weren't there. By the end of my 48-hour binge, I was drained of all energy and emotion, lying on the floor of my apartment at the Château Lincoln, staring up at the ceiling and feeling like I was going to die. I hadn't slept for three days, or maybe it was five. I had honestly lost count. I was afraid to give into the exhaustion. If I went to sleep, I feared I might never wake up. As one of my favorite bands, Chicago, once asked, "Does anybody really know what time it is?" Well, back in those days, I often had no clue.

We had a game that Tuesday night, and the Expos needed me. But I needed another fix to get me back on my feet. That meant my team would have to wait, because in the summer of 1982, everything took a backseat to cocaine, even the game I loved.

As the walls of my apartment closed in on me, cocaine consumed me both in body and in spirit. The ringing of the phone awakened me from my trance. Somehow I rolled across the room and managed to pick it up. Most junkies would have just ignored the call. I didn't realize it at the time, but my effort to reach the phone meant I wanted help.

The call came from someone in the Expos front office who was wondering where the hell I was because our game against the Mets was about to start. I can't tell you who placed the call because junkies aren't the most detail-oriented people on the planet. What I do know is that the fear of having my secret exposed momentarily jolted me to my senses. I muttered something about a case of food poisoning, a terrible headache, and problems of a...umm...personal nature, hoping that one of those excuses would stick.

When I think back to that night, it's with a mixture of embarrassment and gratitude. I never thought I would, but I ended up falling into a trap that ensnared many baseball players of that era. Years before steroids became baseball's Public Enemy No. 1, coke reigned supreme among certain major-leaguers. Regardless of what city you played in, cocaine could easily be found, for the right price. If you had told me when I broke into the big leagues in 1979 that I would be seduced by the charms of the white powder, I would have just laughed in your face. Prior to making the majors, I never drank, smoked, or did drugs. I barely ever cursed or stayed out late. You might say I was a boring guy. Throughout my life, baseball and other sports had always been my sole passion and focus—my drugs of choice.

Was it a case of too much, too soon? Probably. During the strike-shortened 1981 season, I stole a rookie-record 71 bases in 88 games and hit over .300, becoming one of a select group of players ever to make the All-Star team in his first year. The sportswriters pointed out that the strike had likely cost me a chance to break the modern-day record for steals in a season, 118, which belonged to Lou Brock before Rickey Henderson shattered it in 1982. My overnight success thrust me into the spotlight. A prominent baseball writer went so far as to proclaim that I was helping to revolutionize the game. "In case you've been away for about a decade, baseball has changed," wrote Thomas Boswell of the *Washington Post*. "Fundamentally. It's guys like Tim Raines who have done it." Boswell cited a 1981 game against the Los Angeles Dodgers in which I scored standing up from first base on a routine single to right field. "When Raines gets on, it's as though the groundskeepers accidentally put the bases only 80 feet apart and he's the only one who's found out yet," Boswell continued. That made me feel special. It also made me believe I was untouchable.

If it weren't for Fernando Valenzuela's incredible start in the majors, I would have easily won the National League Rookie of the Year award. And if it weren't for Fernando's Dodgers, the Expos would have reached the World Series in 1981. Maybe a less dramatic start to my career would have resulted in a smoother maturation process. As it stood, there I was, less than two months into my first full season in the big leagues, on the cover of a national sports magazine. The dose of quick success led me to believe that I had it all figured out. Instead of committing myself to taking my play to an even higher level, I took my gifts for granted. After cocaine got a hold of me, it didn't take long for Rock to hit rock bottom.

The problem snowballed quickly, excuse the pun. Playing in a foreign city full of temptation, walking around with an air of invincibility, I succumbed to peer pressure and allowed some of my older teammates to lead me astray. Montreal was a party town, but ironically, I got my first introduction to cocaine back in my sleepy hometown of Sanford, Florida, after my rookie season. I wanted to party like a star. So when some old high school classmates pulled out some coke, I figured, why not? I soon found out that the drug gave me a feeling that bordered on all-powerful.

When I returned to Montreal for the 1982 season, I brought my newly discovered taste for cocaine with me. And that led me to hang out with the wrong group of Expos, the ones who cocaine had firmly in its grips. Some of them had been using the stuff for years. On game days, they'd show up in the clubhouse after a long night of partying, put on their uniforms, and go out and play ball. I didn't think the drugs made them better players, but as far as I could tell, it didn't make their performance suffer, either.

When you're far from home and trying to fit in with your older teammates, it's amazing how quickly you can go down a dangerous path, especially when you have more money in your pocket than you've ever had before. During the off-season, I signed a contract that bumped my pay from $35,000 to $200,000. That kind of cash allowed me to afford the $1,000 a week I spent on cocaine. The possibility of getting hooked didn't cross my mind. As far as I was concerned, I had everything under control and could stop whenever I felt like it. Other people—weaker people—became junkies. Not me. I was very naive.

I tried my best to conceal my behavior from the world. But like any addict, I went to reckless lengths to make sure my habit got fed. On the road, I would meet with shady drug connections I got to know through my teammates. At home, I'd leave cocaine lying around the apartment. My wife at the time, Virginia, got wise to my problem and dumped my stash down the drain on more than one occasion. It worried her a lot. She hoped that I was just going through a phase.

The drug-related anecdote that the media jumped on and elevated into legend involved my tendency to keep cocaine on my person during games, specifically snug against my butt in the back pocket of my uniform. It's undisputed truth that I would sneak a snort in the clubhouse bathroom between innings, but the part about making sure I slid headfirst into bases so as not to break the vial of coke is somewhat exaggerated. Anybody who remembers my style of play knows that I went into bases headfirst long after I stopped carrying coke around with me.

Sometimes in the throes of a post-cocaine crash, I'd doze off in the dugout during games. Fortunately, games back then usually clocked in at around two hours. I probably would have had to lay out a sleeping bag if I had participated in too many marathon games. I learned that summer that when the exhilarating high of a drug wears off, a crippling low sets in. Your body and brain crave more. So you either give them more or you become a physical and mental mess. That's what makes cocaine addiction such a vicious cycle.

Missing that late June game against the Mets ended up being a blessing in disguise. Following the evening wake-up call, the Expos dispatched team doctor Robert Broderick to my apartment to check on me. I told him through the door that I needed to throw some clothes on, and I rushed to the bathroom to get rid of whatever coke I had on hand. The moment I flushed the powder down the toilet, I thought, *What the hell did you do that for?* That's the balancing act of an addict. As much as I wanted to avoid getting caught, I also didn't like the idea of flushing hundreds of dollars' worth of drugs down the john. The doctor didn't need to see the drugs to know I was afflicted by something far worse than food poisoning. I didn't know what to do, and my mind wasn't clear enough to come up with a plan. I felt scared. So I just followed my instincts and confessed what had been going on with me. The next day, I met with team president John McHale. He listened closely as the words came spilling out of my mouth. He didn't get upset. He just took it all in, like an understanding father.

I don't know if my confession surprised the front office or not. In 1982, I tried to maintain the appearance that I was ready to play every day. Though I still put up decent numbers and led the National League in plate appearances, there were times when I felt frozen in place, unable to see balls pitched to or hit at me. Several times, I dove out of the way of pitches that were clearly strikes. One of those times, I dusted myself off and asked the home-plate umpire how close I came to getting hit in the head. "Er, that pitch was right down the middle of the plate, son," the confused ump replied.

I wouldn't have been able to keep my drug habit a secret for much longer. One downside of playing in Canada was that we had to go through customs every time we returned to the country, a process that often included drug-sniffing dogs. Looking back, I'm thankful that I had enough judgment not to transport any narcotics over the border. Otherwise, my problems could have been much worse.

I take full responsibility for my actions. No one put a gun to my head and said, "Hey, snort this." That's why, when asked by team management whether others Expos were taking drugs, I never revealed the names of teammates who I knew were also abusing cocaine. I was a young, up-and-coming player who the Expos had a vested interest in supporting through hard times. Some of the other guys with cocaine problems were at the tail end of their careers, making them more expendable. I didn't want to be the reason that any of them lost their jobs.

To be perfectly clear, the majority of my Expos teammates had nothing to do whatsoever with what a handful of us were doing. Many of them went on to have great careers in baseball, such as Tim Wallach and Terry Francona; Doug Flynn went on to head up the state of Kentucky's anti-drug program. I can only imagine that my non-drug-using teammates noticed a change in me. When you spend almost every day with someone for six months, you pick up on even the slightest behavioral changes. In my case, we were talking about a complete personality transformation. But I was still relatively new to the team, and a lot of my teammates didn't know me that well. Even if they did detect that something was wrong, their instinct may have been to mind their own business. I can't blame them for that.

In 1985, I became the only Montreal player to testify before a Pittsburgh grand jury looking into the cocaine epidemic in Major League Baseball. I had to live with the reality that Tim Raines, the exciting young ballplayer, had been replaced in the public eye by Tim Raines, the recovering coke fiend. It was up to me to choose how I wanted the rest of my career defined. For that reason, confronting my addiction and getting help to beat it represented the most formative chapter of my career. It sped up my maturation process.

Drugs don't free you. They greatly limit you. After I kicked the habit, I vowed to play every game in the most uninhibited manner possible. The only white lines I wanted to see were those on a baseball field. And I didn't want to be confined by the 90 feet between bases. When I reached first base, I wanted every pitcher-catcher combo in the league to know that I was going to take off for second and that there was nothing they could do to keep me from getting there. I would learn to master the art of the stolen base by taking just the right lead and accelerating so quickly that only a perfect throw could get me out. The idea of being a one-dimensional player didn't appeal to me, however. I also wanted to generate runs and knock them in. I wanted to bunt for hits and to drive balls over the fence for home runs. I wanted to track down every ball that came my way in the outfield. And above all, I wanted to have fun. To be that type of player, I needed to give the game my full focus and dedication.

There are a lot of cautionary tales in life and in baseball. Drugs have ruined a lot of careers. A former Expos teammate of mine once approached me at an old-timers' game asking for money to buy drugs. I realized that if things had gone differently, I might have been that guy. Cocaine wasn't just an Expos problem. How great would players like Darryl Strawberry and Dwight Gooden have been if they hadn't struggled with drugs and alcohol? They'd both be in Cooperstown, that much I know. I got to know Darryl and Dwight when we all played for the New York Yankees in the 1990s. As Darryl once told *Sports Illustrated*, "We were young, famous, and rich. Nobody could tell us anything, and they allowed us to do whatever we wanted to. You know, once you cross over to the major leagues, you're supposed to [instantly] become a man, but you're not...You're not a man just because you're 20 years old and in the big leagues. You're still a kid, and you've got a lot to learn about life."

Thankfully, I tackled my problem and moved past it. That turbulent summer of 1982 easily could have had long-term consequences for me. The Expos organization supported me all the way. McHale drove me to twice-a-week therapy sessions during the last months of the season. The Thursday after our last game of the season, the team sent me to a California rehabilitation facility to get clean. My parents flew out west to give me their support. They felt torn up inside by what had happened to me. I had kept my secret hidden from them, meaning they didn't find out about my problem until it became public. My mom and dad thought I had enough sense to stay away from drugs, so at first they felt anger toward me. But as time went on, I think they realized that I deserved credit for trying to atone for my human mistake. After I completed the 30-day program in California, the challenge became staying sober. Without the right support network, it's very possible I would have slipped back into addiction.

The day-to-day process of resisting the temptation of drugs and other vices can be difficult. The man most responsible for ensuring that I stayed on the straight and narrow was my teammate, Andre Dawson, who became a mentor and a great friend as I tried to pick up the pieces of my life and rehabilitate my image. I watched how Andre carried himself as a person and a player and decided that I would follow his lead. Behind his intimidating facade was a person who exuded warmth and kindness. And on the field, he pushed himself to be the best. He and Gary Carter were the hardest-working players I ever saw.

In December 1982, I talked about my addiction in a front-page story in the *Montreal Gazette*. In the article, I opened up about snorting cocaine on stadium grounds, at teammates' apartments, and on team flights. As ashamed as I felt by my actions, I wanted to take ownership of them. My frankness about my problem made me a target of opposing fans over the next several seasons. Montreal played in the same division as the Mets and Phillies, and New York and Philadelphia fans especially liked to taunt me. I didn't let their words get to me. Instead, I let my actions on the field do the talking.

I remained on the wagon for the rest of my career. And I took the lessons of my sophomore season with me everywhere I went for the next two decades, including to youth baseball clinics where I talked about the dangers of drugs. That difficult year made me a better player, teammate, husband, and father. When I first set out to beat the problem, I thought about how my three-year-old son, Tim

Jr., so full of innocence and joy, must have felt when he stared into his father's vacant eyes. I would never let him or anyone else close to me down again.

Now that I've fulfilled an unimaginable dream of becoming a Hall of Famer, I can look back at all the struggles and triumphs of my career with a lot of perspective. So many important chapters in baseball history, some positive and others less so, took place while I was in uniform. I experienced them all and look forward to sharing my reflections with you here.

I played in an era when speed was much more a part of the game. Nowadays, teams mostly go after guys who can hit the ball out of the park. I made my name as a "table setter," a guy who could get on base and put pressure on opposing pitchers and defenses. I relied on the guys hitting behind me to knock me in. Nothing kills the momentum of an inning or irritates the hitters in the middle of a lineup more than a guy getting caught stealing. When I took off for second or third, I was successful nearly 85 percent of the time. You often hear me mentioned in the same breath as Rickey Henderson, baseball's all-time stolen-base leader. If you look at our numbers, we had very similar careers. I didn't have Rickey's oversized personality or proclaim myself to be the greatest. I just followed three simple steps to help my team win: get on base by hit or walk, run up a storm, and cross home plate.

I never could have imagined the satisfaction and joy I derived from my 12 seasons in Montreal, a time during which the Expos proved that they could compete with the best teams in baseball. When the time came to decide which logo would appear on my Hall of Fame plaque, the choice was easy. I will always be an Expo.

When I left Montreal after the 1990 season, I was fortunate to land in Chicago on a White Sox team that benefited from my play and veteran leadership. Despite its outcome, the 1993 American League Championship Series against the Toronto Blue Jays stands out as one of my career highlights. I had an incredible assortment of teammates in Chicago. Some, like Frank Thomas and Robin Ventura, took conventional routes to the majors, and others, like Bo Jackson and Michael Jordan, tried their hand at two sports. The relationships I developed with the White Sox led to a coaching job with the team and gave me a chance to celebrate along with the city in 2005 when the team won its first World Series since 1917.

It was beyond my comprehension to think I'd start the final chapter of my playing career by participating on two World Series–winning teams in New York. That experience gave me an opportunity to pay forward the support I got from older teammates when I was just starting out. I tried to serve as a role model to Derek Jeter and the other young players who would become a part of baseball history with the Yankees.

The more I played, the more I wanted to keep playing. As I neared my 20th season in the big leagues, I learned that a disease called lupus would likely force me into retirement. I had never heard of lupus before, but I got to know it very, very well in a short period of time. The disease caused my immune system to turn against me. But I vowed to beat it and to get back on the baseball field. Eventually I did, and my return paved the way for one of the greatest moments of my career: playing with my son, Tim Jr., in a major league game in 2001.

What I came to learn as a player is that it didn't matter if I was playing in the first, 100th, or 2,500th game of my career—that jittery sensation I felt in the pit of my stomach before a game never went away. Other than during the '82 season, when I wasn't in the proper mindset to make appropriate choices, I never took a single game in my career for granted. As soon as I took the field, the butterflies always went away. The baseball diamond was home to me.

You never know where life will take you. I don't claim to have all the answers, but I hope my story helps inspire you in your own life. Every team I played on had guys who were at each other's throats for one reason or another, but I prided myself on steering clear of clubhouse dissension. I've always thought that if you couldn't get along with me, you couldn't get along with anybody. I didn't care where someone came from or whether our personalities clicked. All that mattered was that we respected one another and the uniform we wore. I had an incredible baseball journey. Along the way, I learned a lot about myself, life, and the game that gave me so much. I take an enormous amount of pride in what I accomplished during my 23 years in the game. Major league baseball fields were my playgrounds, and I enjoyed every moment of playing the game.

CHAPTER TWO

2

A LOT OF GREAT BASEBALL PLAYERS have come from the state of Florida, but only a handful attended my alma mater, Seminole High School, in Sanford. Of the four who reached the big leagues, two are named Raines. A third is former All-Star and World Series MVP David Eckstein. You might say Seminole specialized in producing little guys with big hearts.

My parents, Ned Sr. and Florence, grew up in a rural county in south-central Georgia. And that's where they met and married. But after my dad's older brother told him about plentiful job opportunities in Florida, he moved my mom and older brother there in 1957 and found construction work. He was 20 years old at the time. It turned out to be a smart move. Sixty years later, he and my mom are still living together in Florida.

I came along about three years after my parents moved away from Georgia. I remember the Sanford of my youth as an idyllic place, but that's probably because I lived in something of a cocoon. I didn't have many friends growing up. I didn't need any, because I spent almost all of my free time with my four brothers, three who were older than me and one who was younger. We lived in the same green, three-bedroom house our entire childhoods, with all five boys sharing a bedroom for a number of years. It was a tight squeeze that required one of us, usually the youngest, to sleep on the floor. My parents couldn't afford to buy all of us the newest sneakers or latest fashions, but we weren't poor by any means. My mom helped boost our household income by cleaning houses. In our home, clothes and footwear got handed down from the top to the bottom, a system that never left us wanting.

For the duration of my childhood, you'd only find me at my house at meals and bedtime. All of my other waking hours were spent playing organized sports or pickup games with my brothers and friends. Because my mom didn't have the opportunity to spend a lot of quality time with her sports-obsessed children and hard-working husband, she made a point of making sure we all sat down for supper together. Me and my brothers loved to eat, and my mom cooked up some of the best soul food around every night. Collard greens, cornbread, fried chicken, green beans, and sweet potato pie were my favorites, and I had to get to the table early if I wanted to get my fair share. There was a lot of competition for that food.

I didn't get into much trouble as a kid, so the rare times that I did misbehave stick out in my memory. When I was six or seven years old, I learned the hard way that adult habits didn't appeal to me. My parents smoked, and in a misguided attempt to emulate them, I helped myself to one of their cigarettes and brought it to school with me. Before entering the building, I took a drag and immediately went into a coughing fit that seemed to last the rest of the day. That was the last time I attempted to smoke a cigarette.

My older brothers and my father, who played semipro baseball, served as my athletic role models. In one all-star game of my childhood, my brothers and I formed the entire infield. It may have been one of the games that my father volunteered to umpire, though he refused to call balls and strikes in any games we played in. The local newspaper took note of our family ties, publishing stories about our exploits with headlines like WHEN IT RAINES, IT POURS.

In my eyes, my second-oldest brother, Levi, was the greatest athlete who ever walked the planet. And for a while, it looked like Levi had the best chance of any Raines son to reach the major leagues. My father thought Ned, who hit for a lot more power than me, had the most potential, however. He went as far as to tell our high school baseball coach that he would buy him dinner if Ned wasn't the first of his sons to make it to the majors. In 1975, Levi signed a free-agent contract with the Minnesota Twins. He hit no lower than .281 in his three seasons in the Twins system before suffering a career-ending knee injury. Ned, who played baseball at Seminole Community College, got drafted in the second round by the San Francisco Giants. He posted good numbers in the minors, but unfortunately, he had trouble with his eyes and had to retire before getting a shot at the majors.

For decades, there were two high schools in Sanford, one for white kids and one for black kids. Seminole High School had been integrated back in the mid-1960s but not in any kind of large-scale way. It wasn't until I got to high school in the mid-1970s that it saw a real influx of black students. Being around a lot of white kids wasn't anything new to me, however. For as long as I could remember, I had played on mostly white baseball teams in and around the area.

Ned, who was a year older than me, and I were usually the only black kids on the team.

The only time I remember being aware of my race on the baseball field was when my team played a team down the road in Lake Mary, Florida. At some point during the game, I heard someone shout out a racial slur. I don't know who it was directed at, but by process of elimination, I figured it had to be me and my brother. I'm sure the incident rattled my mother, who chauffeured us around in the family station wagon and worked the concession stand or served as scorekeeper at many of our games. She grew up in an era when people frequently uttered hateful words. My parents shielded my siblings and me as much as possible from the ugly realities of racism, preferring to raise us with love in our hearts. We knew some white people didn't like black people, but we didn't really understand why.

If you've seen *42*, the movie about Jackie Robinson's historic career, then you saw some not-so-flattering scenes of my hometown. After the Brooklyn Dodgers signed Jackie in 1945, they assigned him to their Triple A affiliate, the Montreal Royals, who trained in Sanford. From the moment Jackie reported to camp, the locals treated him with hostility. That's actually an understatement. The residents of Sanford, shocked that the Dodgers had signed a black player, literally ran him off the field. I was well into adulthood before I learned about this unfortunate chapter in Sanford's history. But racial tensions in Sanford seem still to persist. Most of you remember the 2012 incident in which 17-year-old Trayvon Martin was shot and killed by a man named George Zimmerman while walking through a Sanford neighborhood. The story got a huge amount of media coverage and provoked a national debate over race relations across the country. It's amazing to think that more than half a century after Jackie's run-in with the locals in Sanford that we're still trying to figure out how to get along with each other.

My father experienced bigotry firsthand. The "colored only" water coolers and restrooms and the nasty comments directed at black people became a part of everyday life. He decided early on that the best weapon against racism was success. So he put his head down and set out to do the best job he could. He started out as a general laborer for a construction company, making $1 an hour, but soon got promoted to road grader despite the opposition of the all-white co-workers on that crew. My dad's bosses at Hubbard Construction recognized his skill and work ethic and rewarded him appropriately. Good for them. For the next 40 years, he did the company proud.

One of my favorite childhood memories is of my brothers and me having foot races with my dad on the dirt road in front of our house. At least once per week, we'd all line up and run to a telephone pole about 100 yards down the road. By the time I reached my teenage years, my dad had put together an undefeated streak that spanned well over a decade. He took pride in not letting us beat him. Then one day when I was 13 or 14, I told him, "Come on, Pops. I think I can get you today." And sure enough, I proceeded to edge him out for the first time ever. After working 10 hours that day, he wasn't in the best condition to run, but to his credit, he didn't shy away from the challenge. After the race, he smiled and congratulated me… and never raced us again. I think he realized the torch had been passed. When I became a father, I started the same tradition with my sons—but I learned from my dad's experience. When Tim Jr., who we also called "Little Rock," started getting close to beating me, I stopped racing him.

That road we had so much fun running down was also the scene of the worst moment of my childhood. In 1968, my four-year-old sister, Anita Gail, the youngest of the seven Raines children, was walking along the side of the road with a couple of my siblings when a driver lost control of his car and veered off the road, hitting and killing her. I was at home at the time, waiting for my siblings to return from a nearby convenience store with candy. Instead, I heard sirens.

The days following my sister's death were filled with tears, sorrow, and incredible emotion. Everyone was a mess. I couldn't make sense of it. I remember being in a state of disbelief. How could my little sister be gone just like that? I peeked into the bedroom that she shared with my other sister, Patricia, expecting her smiling face to greet me. From that day forward, every time I ran or walked down that road, I thought of Anita Gail. As I got older, her death reminded me that every day is a blessing, because you just never know when tragedy is going to strike and change everything.

Sports gave me a refuge from the sadness of that incident. My greatest passion as a kid was football. When I closed my eyes at night, I didn't picture myself on a major league baseball field. No, I had gridiron dreams. I was a sophomore in high school when O.J. Simpson broke the single-season NFL rushing record in 1973, topping the 2,000-yard mark with the Buffalo Bills. As a running back at Seminole, I routinely ripped off runs of 20, 30, and 40 yards. My low center of gravity made it hard for tacklers to bring me down. Nothing satisfied me more than slicing through the defense and taking the ball over the goal line for six points. My teammates nicknamed me "Little Juice," and wearing uniform No. 32, just like O.J., I set my sights on becoming every bit the force of nature that he was. Unfortunately, O.J.'s life took him in an unforeseen direction that changed how people view him. I prefer to remember him the way he was.

With the right opportunities, I saw no reason why I couldn't become one of the greatest rushers of all time. I didn't have the same kind of relationship with baseball. I liked playing the game and occasionally watched Braves games on the TBS Superstation, but as a young kid, I didn't have a favorite player or even anyone I strived to emulate. Maybe that explains why I never imagined myself becoming a professional baseball player.

By my early teens, I had developed into one of the biggest kids around. My high school football coach tried to get me in the weight room, but I resisted that chore at all costs. The idea of repeatedly lifting iron barbells over my head just didn't appeal to me. I stayed in game shape by sprinting and stretching and by just playing the games. I was blessed with good genetics. My father and all of his sons lacked great size, but we all had athletic bodies.

As a teenager, I was one growth spurt away from becoming an absolute physical specimen. Unfortunately, a last bump in height and bulk eluded me, and by my senior year of high school, I was no bigger than I was as a freshman. That, I realized, put a serious dent in my future plans to dominate the NFL. I still had a rock-solid physique, an attribute that later earned me my nickname, but I no longer resembled a man among boys.

In addition to football and baseball, I also played basketball and ran track. My baseball coach didn't mind me double dipping on spring sports, on the condition that I only competed in track meets on days when we didn't have a baseball game. I never practiced running. I just went out to the track and did it. For a while, I held the long-jump record at Seminole. I ran hurdles, too. Most importantly, I met a girl named Virginia Hilton on the track team. She and I started dating and, in 1979, became husband and wife.

I kept my grades up throughout high school, and during my junior year, I signed a letter of intent to play football for Doug Dickey at the University of Florida, the college program I had rooted for growing up. I realized I'd probably ride the pine for my first couple of years in Gainesville, and my conversations with Coach Dickey indicated that when I finally did see the field, I'd probably be lined up as a wide receiver. To this day, I can't figure out why no colleges wanted me to play baseball for them. The area had a bunch of top-flight programs: Florida, Florida State, and Miami, to name just a few. But like my future Montreal Expos teammate Andre Dawson, who played his high school ball in Miami, I drew no interest from any of them. Andre ended up taking his talents to Florida A&M University, where he showed college scouts across the state and country what an enormous oversight they'd made. The Expos took him in the 11th round of the 1975 draft, and two years later, he took home National League Rookie of the Year honors.

Whatever the reason for the recruiters' disinterest in us, history will show that two of the best players to ever wear Expos uniforms apparently weren't good enough to play Division I college baseball.

The colleges overlooked me, but at least one major league team expressed serious interest in me and Ned. During my junior year of high school, a scout for the Los Angeles Dodgers invited us to a tryout. Following the workout, the scout told me he thought the Dodgers would be smart to take me in the first round out of high school. In retrospect, I think he was just flattering me—and it worked. The possibility of being a first-round draft pick by one of baseball's most famous organizations thrilled me, so much so that I decided to concentrate all of my efforts in my last year of high school on baseball. That meant not playing football. During my junior year, I sprained my ankle during a football game. With the possibility of playing professional baseball looming on the horizon, I couldn't afford to sustain another injury.

My father, who was blessed with common sense and a practical view of the world, fully supported my decision. I knew he had a stronger will than I did, so after I told him in the spring of my plan to sit out the upcoming football season, I added, "Whatever I do or say, don't let me near a football field this fall."

My dad wanted more than anything for his children to have opportunities he had missed out on during a lifetime of working his fingers to the bone. He knew that sports represented a path to a better life, and while he realized that making it as a pro athlete was far from guaranteed, he thought his sons should at least have the chance to pursue that goal. The realities of having to provide for a growing family forced him to give up his dream of going professional, but he still found time to play the game he loved, suiting up in the 1950s and '60s for a local baseball team called the Sanford Giants, an integrated team that featured mostly black players. Some of my father's teammates had played minor league ball, so the level of competition was pretty high. I remember how excited I was to go to his games when I was younger. His team played on Tuesday and Saturday nights. Some of the games took place 30 or more miles from my house, which forced my dad to change into his baseball uniform at work and drive all the way to the game. But it was worth it to him. He loved baseball.

During the week (and on some weekends), he worked for Hubbard Construction, and depending on whether my family needed something, like a new car or washing machine, he supplemented his income by picking oranges in the fruit groves or working in a packing house. I really believe that my father would have had a chance to play professional baseball if he had been able to concentrate on that dream. Instead he and my mom started a family and had seven kids together. That meant having to put food on plates and clothes on backs for all of us. My father ended up settling for semipro games in the area. I knew he had put aside his own goals to make sure our family had everything we needed, and I wanted to make him proud.

True to my word, I missed spring football practice and resisted the urge to contact any of the football coaches over the summer. Then I made a huge mistake: I attended Seminole's opening game of the season as a spectator. I had never watched a game from that vantage point, and the atmosphere in the stands thrilled me, causing me to flash back to the two years I had spent busting through opposing defenses as an all-state running back. During my junior year, Ned and I formed a potent one-two combination in the backfield. Ned was about my size, standing 5-foot-8 and weighing about 160 pounds. But, man, could he block! He didn't care if an opposing linebacker had six inches and 40 pounds on him. He'd stick his helmet in the guy's shoulder pad and open up a nice lane for me to run through. With Ned leading the way, I knew no one could touch me. With me cheering in the stands that late summer night, Seminole edged out the opponent by a single point. I spent the entire rest of the night and next day thinking, *Man, I need to find a way to get back out there.*

That Sunday, I approached my dad, who was outside doing yard work. For about two hours, I followed him around, barely saying a word. As he watered the plants, mowed the lawn, and trimmed the shrubs, he didn't say much, either, but it must have been obvious to him that I had something on my mind. I just couldn't work up the nerve to tell him that I wanted to reverse course and play football.

Everyone at school, including all of the coaches, knew how much I loved football. The next day at school, Seminole's running backs coach increased my level of agony by letting me know that there was still a spot on the team for me if I changed my mind. I told him about my earlier conversation with my father before politely declining. The coach gave an understanding nod and asked if it would be okay if he went to talk to my father. After school that day, the coach came over to plead his case. I stood in the background as my father stood unmoved by the coach's words.

"He told me he didn't want to play, and I agreed that was a good idea," my dad said. "I don't think he should play. Too much to lose."

That night before bed, I mustered up the courage to talk to my dad myself.

"It's my senior year, Dad," I started, "and I think I'm making a mistake by not being a part of something that's made me so happy."

He wasn't accustomed to seeing me take such a strong stance. I always did what I was told and rarely challenged my parents' authority. He looked me up and down for a long while before sighing and giving me the okay to play football.

The head football coach had me ask the rest of the team for permission to rejoin them. They consented. I made my season debut in the second half of our second game and, without Ned leading the way this time, proceeded to run for three touchdowns in what turned out to be an undefeated season for the team and an 18-touchdown season for me. My biggest athletic disappointment in high school came when our team had to forfeit two regular seasons wins because one of our players was declared academically ineligible, a development that deprived us of the chance to compete in the state playoffs. The day my principal announced the news in the high school gymnasium was one of the saddest in my life. I viewed the playoffs as a reward for a successful regular season. As I got older, my enthusiasm for playing in the postseason never dimmed.

I skipped playing basketball my senior year and focused on making sure major league scouts noticed me. That June, the Dodgers didn't follow through on their scout's suggestion to draft me in the first round of the 1977 amateur draft. They instead took pitcher Bob Welch, who went on to win 211 major league games, with the 20th overall pick. The first three picks in the entire draft were Harold Baines (White Sox), Bill Gullickson (Expos), and Paul Molitor (Brewers). All put together great careers. Molitor is in the Hall of Fame.

Back then, the draft wasn't televised, so I had no option other than to wait for our home phone to ring. And when it finally did, it wasn't someone from the Dodgers on the other end. The call came from the Montreal Expos, who despite never making their interest in me known, had caught enough of a glimpse of me to pick me with the second pick of the fifth round. (Seeing as I was the first non-pitcher drafted by the Expos that year, I've jokingly referred to myself over the years as a No. 1 pick.) The only association I had with the Expos came from having watched them play a spring training game in Daytona Beach during my senior year of high school. Before their game against the Twins, I approached several players and asked for autographs. Andre Dawson's response to my request became a running joke between us. In my version of the story, Hawk shot me one of his trademark scowls and barked, "Go away, kid!" He doesn't remember the incident but, as he wrote in the foreword to this book, claims he never would have treated a young autograph seeker so rudely. He's probably right, but in the absence of proof like a crumpled old autograph from Andre, I'll stick to my story.

After the Expos drafted me, a scout named Bill Adair, the same guy who signed Andre at his Miami home, came to my house to talk with my parents and me about signing a contract. The assessment of me by the Dodgers scout had elevated my hopes. Hearing that a scout believes you're one of the 20 best players in the country is a real confidence booster. It's a little harder to know where you stand when you get drafted in the fifth round.

Adair told me that the Expos organization loved my speed. He knew I had stolen home more than 10 times in high school. He also praised my skills as a shortstop, but he informed me that I had the body of a second baseman. My family and I listened to everything

Adair had to say. Later that night, I discussed my two immediate options with my parents. I could enroll at the University of Florida and try to play both football and baseball there, or I could go into the Expos minor league system. But there was a middle ground, too. Adair mentioned that the Expos would pay for me to go to college if things didn't work out. That clinched it. I signed with the Expos and decided to give myself two or three years to prove whether I had enough talent to make the major leagues.

My signing bonus with the Expos was around $20,000, not including the provision for college tuition. I rested easy after signing the deal, knowing that if I didn't have what it took as a baseball player, I could go to college and try to become the next 2,000-yard back in the NFL.

Obviously, I never ended up in a college classroom, let alone a college backfield. But I never abandoned my running back instincts while playing baseball. The thing I loved most about playing high school football in Florida was the hoopla and the electricity of the 10,000 or more fans who packed stadiums on Friday nights to watch a game. And I sought in my own way to make baseball a faster, more intense experience for myself and the fans. I equated stealing a base with rushing for a first down. Whenever I dashed around the bases, I felt the same thrill I had when scoring a touchdown. As a high school baseball player, I didn't experience the fan feedback I would later get as a professional, mostly because we didn't have many fans coming out to see us. But when I got to the minor leagues, I saw how much people embraced my style of play, cheering like crazy every time I used my legs to give the team an edge. The roar of the fans helped fuel and sustain me during my career. From day one, my philosophy was to try and put the ball in play and never to strike out more times than I walked. I attribute my successes to that simple recipe.

By the time I signed a professional contract, I had started following baseball more closely, looking for players I could pattern myself after. Joe Morgan of the Cincinnati Reds quickly became my role model. A two-time National League MVP and perennial Gold Glove winner, he hit for a high average and stole a lot of bases. Plus, like me, he didn't cut an imposing figure. He, too, was a smurf, standing 5-foot-7 and weighing 160 pounds. I started rooting for the Reds because of Joe and his Big Red Machine teammate, Pete Rose, whose talent and enthusiasm I admired. If the Expos thought I'd make a good second baseman, I would aspire to model myself after the best.

I honestly didn't know what to expect when I entered the Expos farm system. And the feeling from the organization was probably mutual. The first thing that the player development guys instructed me to do when I reported to rookie ball in Sarasota was to learn to switch-hit. They told me that a player with speed like mine could beat out a lot of hits if he stood one step closer to first base when leaving the batter's box. That made sense, but the assignment still intimidated me. Imagine reporting for your first day at a new job and being informed you immediately needed to learn a major new skill. Well, that's how I felt. Throughout Little League and high school, I had only batted from the right side of the plate. I couldn't imagine what it would feel like to swing any other way. But I learned on the fly, utilizing the two weeks before the start of the Gulf Coast League season to get comfortable hitting left-handed.

I look back at the 1977 season in Sarasota as a pivotal one. It represented the first time in my entire life that I was on my own. Though only two and a half hours from home, I felt like I had landed on another planet. I was no longer Tim Raines, the four-sport star athlete and big fish in a little pond. I was just a 17-year-old kid trying to make it as a professional ballplayer, surrounded by a bunch of other young players with the same goal. I had no idea where I stood in comparison with the other guys embarking on that same journey. No longer just playing for the fun of it anymore, I now had a six-day-a-week job that involved getting up early and trying to impress the people who showed enough faith in me to draft me. It was hot under the Sarasota sun, and sometimes it didn't feel so enjoyable, but I committed myself to showing how good I could be, both at the plate and as a second baseman.

Due to most pitchers throwing right-handed, the majority of my at-bats at rookie ball and the seasons that followed came from the left side. I took to the new skill pretty quickly, hitting .280 in Sarasota. Just as the coaches had hoped, I beat out a decent number of infield hits. But it took me a couple of years to generate any kind of power as a left-handed hitter. My first home run as a professional didn't come until my third year of pro ball.

When I was just starting out, I didn't realize how difficult it is to become a major league ballplayer. All the guys I shared a clubhouse with in Sarasota had been stars at their respective high schools and colleges. But of the 37 players who suited up for Sarasota that year, only three reached the majors. And the two besides me didn't stay there very long. As a team, we basically stunk, winning only 19 of 54 games. I got a tremendous education that summer, however. Everyone quickly found out how well I could run, and I did a lot of it in the minors. In rookie ball, I stole 29 bases in 31 attempts. But in my new role as a switch-hitter, I also showed I could handle myself with the bat. The Expos thought they were getting a speedster, but my early performance indicated they might be getting much more.

I experienced further success the next season in the Florida State League, where I hit .287 for the Expos affiliate in West Palm Beach. I was focusing so much on my hitting that season that I, no pun intended, took a step back on the base paths. Yes, I swiped 57 bags, but I also got caught 21 times, the highest number of unsuccessful attempts I had in any season as a professional.

By my second year in the Expos system, I felt very comfortable. You hear all the time about teams or organizations that have family-like atmospheres, but in our case, that sentiment rang true. On the road, we'd use a local motel as a base of operation before night games. Minor league travel budgets are tight, so it wasn't uncommon to see 20 players packed into a tiny room before a game, telling stories and joking around. We all had the same goal of making the majors, but that didn't prevent us from feeling loyalty toward each other as we competed to earn promotions to the next level.

In 1979, I got called up to Double A Memphis, where I showed some pop in my bat for the first time. Five home runs may not seem like a lot, but it was five more than I had hit in my first two seasons in the minors. I also hit 25 doubles and 10 triples that season.

As the season drew to a close, I assumed I'd soon be on my way back home to Florida. I really didn't think I had a chance to get called up to the big leagues in September, and quite honestly, I had other things on my mind at the time. At the end of August, Virginia gave birth to our son, Tim Jr. That was a beautiful moment that made me feel very blessed.

Some of the players on the Memphis Chicks team knew they were going to get promoted to Montreal when major league rosters expanded, and for that reason, a few of them couldn't wait until the Southern League season ended. I had a different take on the situation. Memphis qualified for the playoffs, and I wanted to devote my full attention to helping my team win a championship, even if it was "only" a Double A championship. After playing for teams with losing records my first two years as a pro, it felt good to represent a winner.

Facing elimination in the series, we trailed the Nashville Sounds by a run in the top of the ninth inning. I drew a walk and proceeded to steal second base, third base, and home to tie a game that we went on to win. Our season ended the next day when we lost to the Sounds, but I felt good knowing that I had played to win. As my dad always told me, "You go all the way or you don't go at all."

To my surprise, I did get the call to Montreal in early September. For a young guy who hadn't yet turned 20, entry into the big leagues represented the second major milestone in my life in a single week. Life was happening fast. The Expos were just half a game out of first place in the National League East when I got promoted, meaning all of the games left on the schedule had significance. In the clubhouse, I was surrounded by stars like Tony Perez and emerging stars like Andre Dawson and Gary Carter. I knew of these guys, but I didn't really know them on any kind of personal level. Ellis Valentine, an exciting young outfielder for the Expos, invited me to live with him when I got called up to Montreal. I appreciated the gesture and took him up on his offer.

I knew I'd have a very limited role during the final month of the season, but that didn't keep me from having a serious case of the nerves. I felt out of place in a major league stadium. During batting practice, I had a difficult time shagging fly balls. I'd line them up, get under them, and prepare to make the catch, only to find the ball fall 10 feet behind me. My veteran teammates got a good laugh out of that, of course.

I remember how apprehensive I felt when I jogged onto the field at Olympic Stadium on September 11, 1979, to make my major league debut, against the Cubs. My dad had driven all the way from Florida to Montreal to attend the game. For a while, it looked like he might have to wait another day or two to see me take the field. Through six innings, I remained on the bench. But after Carter opened the bottom of the seventh inning with a single, manager Dick Williams called on me to pinch-run. In some ways, it was the best of all possible debuts. The Expos held a comfortable 7–2 lead, so it wasn't a stealing situation. All I had to do was avoid getting picked off or making a stupid base-running blunder. To be safe, I stayed closer to first base than I did at any other time in my entire major league career. I quickly got erased on a 6-4-3 double play.

I went on to make five more pinch-running appearances that season, stealing the first two bases of my major league career. It made my dad so happy to be in the stands for those games, though he felt a little disoriented by all the people at Olympic Stadium chattering away in French. He knew a good chunk of the earth spoke a different language, but he never expected to hear anything but English or Spanish at a baseball game. The sight and sound of so many French speakers really entertained him, to the point where he would just stare at the people having conversations around him.

The Expos ended up falling short of making the playoffs in 1979, losing out on the last weekend of the season to Willie Stargell, Dave Parker, and the Pittsburgh Pirates. To this day, some of us can't stand to hear Sister Sledge's "We Are Family," which became the unofficial anthem for the '79 Pirates as they went all the way and beat the Baltimore Orioles in the World Series. A lot of players from the '79 Expos are quick to point out that we played eight doubleheaders in the month of September, an unusual turn of events necessitated by several weather-related postponements earlier in the year. When you're trying to sprint to the finish line at the end of a long season, that kind of scheduling nightmare can wreak havoc with your pitching staff.

Still, 1979 represented a major breakthrough for the Expos, who until that point hadn't had a winning season in franchise history. In a relatively short time, the team's ownership had built an excellent team pretty much from the ground up. Plus, reinforcements were on the way. Guys like starting pitcher Bill Gullickson and myself had just arrived in the big leagues. Others, like third baseman Tim Wallach, were about to get promoted to the majors.

As former first-round draft picks in 1977 and 1979 respectively, Gully and Eli (as in the actor, Eli Wallach), carried a heavier weight of expectations. The only way for a team like the Expos to stay competitive in the new free-agent era was to produce a lot of homegrown talent. And the Expos didn't whiff very often when it came to picking players in the first round. Steve Rogers, the team's longtime ace, and outfielder Warren Cromartie, part of the heart and soul of the Expos for a long time, also got selected in the opening round. Then there were later-round picks like Gary Carter (third), Andre Dawson (11th), pitchers Scott Sanderson (third) and Charlie Lea (ninth), and me (fifth)—our long-term success in the majors made the Expos front office look very smart. It's amazing how many key contributors to the Expos of that era got overlooked by other teams. Larry Parrish is a great example. Larry, an All-Star in 1979 and the team's third baseman for many years, went undrafted out of high school and community college.

Our scouts deserved a lot of the credit for the development of our strong farm system. Scouts like Adair and Mel Didier, working under the supervision of scouting director Danny Menendez, went out and found great athletes who were turned into polished ballplayers by our minor league instructors. And the scouting department fanned out all over the country. In Florida, they found players like Cro, Andre, and me. Closer to Montreal, they discovered players like David Palmer, an upstate New Yorker and 21st-round pick in 1976 who did a lot for us when he reached the majors.

Despite just missing the postseason in '79, it was an exciting time for me, the team, and the city of Montreal. You could feel something was brewing. Montreal had become a popular destination for Americans looking for an international experience close to home at a time when the U.S. dollar was very strong. Movie stars and other celebrities flocked to the city, making it one of the disco capitals of the world. Montreal was on fire, and my teammates and I fed off the energy in the streets, at the ballpark, even in the Metro stations. Our goal was to bring a baseball championship to Canada, a milestone we all knew would solidify the popularity of our sport in a country where hockey reigned supreme, understandably so, given the fact that the Montreal Canadiens won four straight Stanley Cups from 1976 to 1979.

My opportunity to contribute to the cause would have to wait another season. I spent most of the 1980 season at Triple A Denver, where I tore up the American Association with a .354 average and 77 stolen bases. Maybe the altitude in Denver helped pad my numbers a little bit, but I think my breakthrough was mostly attributable to developing full confidence in my abilities.

That team, which finished with a record of 92–44, is considered one of the best teams in minor league history. The Bears roster provided a glimpse into the future of the Expos. Gullickson went 6–2 in Triple A with a sub-2.00 ERA before getting called up to Montreal, where he finished the season with 10 major league wins. Gully would eventually play six seasons with the Expos, winning 72 games. (He is also the pitcher *against* whom I probably had the most success in my career; during his time with the Cincinnati Reds and Detroit Tigers, I hit .383 against him with five home runs.) Third baseman Wallach, who went directly from college to Double A, made Triple A pitchers look like they were Little Leaguers, blasting 36 homers and knocking in 124 runs. Tim and I went on to become the only players to wear Expos uniforms for the entire decade of the 1980s. He and I remain great friends to this day. The biggest offensive star for Denver that season was Randy Bass, a slugging first baseman who had 37 home runs and 143 RBIs. The Expos traded him to the Padres at the end of the '80 season, but his major league career never took off. He became a superstar in Japan, however. You may remember him as the guy who came within a home run of breaking the Japanese League's single-season home-run record of 55. The league apparently didn't want a non-Japanese player to break the record, so Bass received a lot of intentional walks in the final games of the 1985 season.

My performance in Denver earned me a couple of call-ups to the Expos, and this time around I actually got to swing a bat. My first career at-bat came against Nolan Ryan. I worked a 3-2 count against Ryan, who then tried to freeze me with a curveball instead of coming in with a heater. It worked. I stood at the plate with the bat on my shoulder and took strike three. I felt the pitch was borderline at best. After I got rung up, I turned to home-plate umpire Paul Runge and told him I thought the pitch was a little low. Runge looked at me like I was crazy. He couldn't believe a guy who had a grand total of zero at-bats prior to this one would question his call. "Go sit down," he told me. I complied. For the record, I still think the pitch was low.

In the sixth inning against reliever Bert Roberge, I hit a ball that bounced high off home plate and beat it out for a single. It wasn't a thing of beauty, but it still counted as my first career major league hit. It also ended up being my *only* hit that season. After crushing almost everything thrown at me in Triple A, I struggled to figure out big league pitching. In 20 at-bats in 1980, I got that one lone infield single.

That season was also the first time I made an impression with Expos manager Dick Williams. Nothing I did as a pinch runner the previous year caught Dick's attention. Dick was very intense and liked for things to be done just so, from spring training until the end of the season. During a game in July 1980, Dick called on me to advance a runner to second base with a bunt. I did as I was instructed and successfully executed a sacrifice fielded by the first baseman. I jogged back to the dugout, expecting Dick to praise me for my bunt, or at the very least, to say nothing. Instead, he got up in my face and yelled, "When we ask you to bunt, we want you to bunt toward third base!" For a 19-year-old, this kind of scolding was scarring. For days afterward, I was afraid Dick really disliked me. Only later did I come to understand that was just his way. Asked once about his tendency to fly off the handle, Dick said, "I don't want to mellow. I'd rather be known as a winner and a poor loser."

That incident rattled my confidence enough to make me think that I'd have a difficult time playing for Dick. But from that point on, we never had any problems with each other. That being said, I'm not sure I ever felt fully relaxed as long as he was in command.

My disorientation at the plate carried over to my life outside the walls of Olympic Stadium, where I was confronted by a whole new culture and a population who didn't speak the same language as me. It took some time to acclimate. Most people in Montreal were bilingual, but I think some French speakers got offended when a visitor or seasonal worker didn't even attempt to speak French. Those who didn't mind speaking English often did so with a thick accent that was hard to understand. At restaurants, I would attempt to order meals in English only to get blank stares in return. Sometimes my order was based entirely on what words on the menu I could understand. Even in Italian restaurants, with the exception of words like "pasta," the menus were written in French, leaving me to wonder what kind of pasta I was getting. At the grocery store, or *epicerie*, all the signs were in French, forcing my wife to work her way through the aisles until she found the items she needed.

We tried to make ourselves as comfortable as possible in Montreal. Sometimes, however, when we felt we needed a taste of home during the season, we'd drive over the border into New York to fill our trunk with American groceries, even though that meant we had to pay a duty on them upon our return to Canada. It was worth every penny in my mind. Having grown up in the American South, Virginia and I enjoyed traditional southern cooking. The supermarket shelves in Plattsburgh, New York, weren't exactly stocked with soul food ingredients, but we found a number of items that just weren't available in Montreal grocery stories. I'm told you can get some pretty good soul food in Montreal these days, but back then, that wasn't the case.

But all of that was okay. The people of Montreal didn't have to conform to our way of doing things. They had their own customs and a wonderful sense of community. Over the course of time, I learned the essentials like *bonjour* and *merci beaucoup*. I felt it was only right to respect the culture I was living in. All I asked in return was that Montrealers continue to support and take pride in the Expos.

After the '80 season, there was nowhere to go but up. Or in my case, down…to play winter ball in Latin America.

The months I spent playing for Expos coach Felipe Alou in Escogido, Dominican Republic, really paved the way for what came later. After my disappointing initiation to the big leagues, I really needed to know where I stood. Facing a lot of big league pitchers in the D.R., I found my timing at the plate and had a productive winter. I also had fun playing in a country where baseball was hands-down the favorite sport. Every game was like a party, with music, dancing girls, and passionate fans. Alou led us to a championship, and on the heels of that experience, I felt I could handle whatever came my way. My dream of running for 2,000 yards on an NFL field would have to remain unfulfilled. Baseball was my future, and I was all-in.

CHAPTER THREE

3

AFTER EXPOS LEFT FIELDER RON LᴇFLORE signed as a free agent with the Chicago White Sox, the Expos decided that I would be his replacement, both in left field and in the leadoff spot in the lineup. That sounded good to me, except for one thing: up until that point, I had only played the outfield once, in the Expos' final game of the 1980 season. The rest of the time I played second base. In winter ball, I only saw action at second, the position I exclusively played in the minors.

Realizing that they shouldn't just throw an untested rookie into their outfield, the Expos sent a coach down to Escogido to tutor me on the finer points of playing left field. Before games, I shagged fly balls and fielded grounders, learned to hit the cut-off man, and worked on playing balls hit off the outfield wall. It took a little bit of time to adjust to my new position, but I am convinced that switching to the outfield was the best thing that ever happened to me. I played second base because that's the position the Expos' player development officials thought best suited my physical makeup and skill set. Truth be told, I had always pictured myself as a center fielder, tracking down balls hit into the gap and throwing out runners at the plate. I realized, however, that center field in

Montreal was spoken for. Andre Dawson won his first Gold Glove award at that position in 1980, an honor he would take home for six consecutive years.

In the minors, I worked to become a dependable second baseman, but I never felt totally comfortable there. I enjoyed certain things about playing the infield, like turning double plays, but I found myself working so hard to improve my defense that I sometimes lacked focus at the plate. I booted too many grounders and failed to make some routine plays that are expected of middle infielders. If the Expos thought I could best help the club by remaining at second base, I would have happily done so, but as it turned out, the timing of LeFlore's departure couldn't have been better.

LeFlore was exactly the type of player I aspired to be...and the type of player the Expos expected me to be. In his only season in Montreal, he led the National League with 97 stolen bases, while getting caught only 19 times. Two years earlier he led the American League in steals as a member of the Detroit Tigers. By watching LeFlore, I learned how much speed could impact a game. It would have been a more difficult transition for me if I had been called upon to replace a slugger in left field or a fan favorite who had been with the organization for many years. I knew I could run, and I had every intention of picking up where LeFlore left off.

Many people expected the Expos to compete for the National League East crown in 1981. We had just missed winning the division the previous season, losing two games at Olympic Stadium to the Phillies on the final weekend of the season to give Philadelphia the National League East title. I saw only limited action in that decisive series and looked forward to the opportunity to see my name in the lineup every day. In my limited appearances in a major league uniform, I had struggled to find my rhythm at the plate. The best way to figure out major league pitching was through repetition.

I was the first Expo to come to bat in the '81 season. Facing Jim Bibby of the Pittsburgh Pirates, a 19-game winner the season before, I worked a walk. With Rodney Scott at the plate, I took off for second base and beat the throw from Pirates catcher Steve Nicosia. As I popped up from my slide, I noticed that the ball had squirted into the outfield. I took off for third base, rounded the bag, and kept running. By the time the Pirates outfielder got the ball in, I had crossed home plate for the first run of the season. I truly believe that moment helped jump-start my career.

I came out of the gates strong, starting the season on a 10-game hitting streak, a period that included a four-hit, four-stolen-base performance against the Phillies. The team got off to a great start, too. By the end of April, we were 12–4 and in first place. Three steals against the Dodgers in a game I ended in the 13th inning with a walk-off home run, the first homer of my career, brought my total to 19 consecutive stolen bases without getting caught. That streak ended the next night when, moments after stealing second, Dodgers catcher Mike Scioscia nailed me trying to take third. All good things must come to an end, I guess. "I slipped," I said jokingly when reporters asked me after the game how Scioscia threw me out.

For the first couple of months of the '81 season, I felt like I was walking (and running) on air. There's no other way to describe it. I thought the pressure of playing in the majors would be a lot more intense. Instead, I showed up to the ballpark every day feeling completely relaxed and ready to have fun. I didn't know if I was in a honeymoon period that would soon end, or if I could continue playing at a high level for three, five, or 10 more years. To be honest, I didn't really care. In that moment, everything seemed perfect, and it didn't seem right to question it. I remember the electricity in Olympic Stadium on the May night when Charlie Lea, a former minor league teammate of mine, pitched the first no-hitter in Expos history. I never thought that baseball could give me the adrenaline rush I got from football, but my rookie season proved me wrong.

My arrival on the scene coincided with that of Dodgers pitcher Fernando Valenzuela, the young phenom who won the first eight starts of his major league career—and pitched nine innings in all of them. That's an achievement that will probably never be duplicated. It had been a while since two rookies had made such a dramatic impact on the national pastime. So when the Dodgers came to Montreal for a series in early May, a photographer from *The Sporting News* snapped a picture of Fernando and me together before the game. I had grown accustomed to seeing my photo in the sports pages of the *Montreal Gazette*, but up until that point, I didn't realize that people outside the province of Quebec cared anything about me or the Expos. I knew that fans considered *The Sporting News* one of the best sources of baseball news around, so I felt honored that they wanted to write an article about me. It felt strange in a way, though. The Expos had a lot of great veteran players who deserved attention. But I guess writers like to seize upon what's fresh and new. Imagine my surprise when the photo of Fernando and me clasping hands outside the batting cage at Olympic Stadium graced the front cover of the magazine. The cover story, entitled "Class of the Freshmen," made me feel like I had arrived. As I soon learned, that level of notoriety so early in my career turned out to be a double-edged sword.

In the midst of my breakout rookie season, I still had my critics, most notably my mother. As the person who shuttled my four brothers and me to hundreds of games in our childhood, she had watched so much baseball over the years that she developed a certain expertise. In June, we played a three-game series against the Braves that was broadcast nationally on the TBS Superstation. That gave my parents a rare opportunity to watch me play on television. I'd be lying if I said I didn't want to impress my family. In our sweep of Atlanta, I went 5-for-14 with six runs scored and five stolen bases. My mom called me after the series to tell me how proud she was of me, before adding, "I noticed that you're swinging at some bad pitches. Try not to do that." She and I enjoyed a good laugh over that one.

We fell out of first place in May, but everyone from manager Dick Williams on down felt confident that we would remain in the race until the very end. Then, after a 7–0 win over the Atlanta Braves on June 11, the games suddenly stopped. We were in third place in the division when the work stoppage hit. Because I was contently living in my own little world, I had no idea that the threat of a strike had loomed all season. The whole thing made little sense to me. I was just a 21-year-old rookie making $35,000 a year and having the time of his life playing baseball. What did I know about labor relations? From what I gathered during the weeks the strike lasted, the owners felt that teams losing a player to free agency should be compensated with a player from the free agent's new team. The Major League Baseball Players Association argued that this change to the rules would represent a step backward by making it less likely for teams to sign free agents.

As the two sides tried to work out their differences, I went home to Sanford, Florida, where I played pickup baseball every afternoon with some college kids. Thanks to that *Sporting News* story and the other attention I had received from the media, residents of my hometown now knew me as the local kid who had made it in the major leagues. I think this surprised a lot of people who still thought of me as that kid who ran wild on the high school football field. They didn't know me as a baseball player. That made sense. Only 20 or so people showed up for my high school baseball games, compared to the 10,000 fans who filled the stands at Friday night football games. There was a writer for the local Sanford paper who periodically updated readers on my progress in the minor leagues, but I suspect a lot of people in the community still doubted whether I could succeed in the major leagues. The reception I got back home was awesome. Everywhere I went, somebody congratulated me on my sudden success in the big leagues. I felt like a real big shot.

While the rest of the team went home and tried to stay in shape, Steve Rogers, the ace of our pitching staff and a member of the players negotiating committee along with Bob Boone, Doug DeCinces, and Mark Belanger, attended meetings aimed at breaking the impasse. The dispute between the owners and the players union finally got worked out with some kind of compromise, but not until a large chunk of the season had been lost.

Before the forced break, I was hitting .322 with 50 stolen bases, a level of accomplishment that earned me a spot as a reserve in the All-Star Game, the first post-strike game that took place. I felt incredibly honored to represent the Expos in Cleveland. In the clubhouse before the game, I saw a couple of familiar faces. Andre Dawson was the starting center fielder for the National League and Gary Carter got voted in at catcher. Surrounded by the best players in the game and 72,000 fans in the ballpark, I had to pinch myself to make sure I wasn't dreaming.

Besides Joe Morgan of the Cincinnati Reds, my other favorite player at the time was Kansas City Royals third baseman George Brett, who was making his sixth All-Star appearance in 1981. I had read *The Art of Hitting .300*, a book written by longtime Royals hitting coach Charley Lau, who helped turn Brett into one of the great hitters in the game. When I came out of the clubhouse for pregame warm-ups, I saw Brett out on the field talking to some of his American League teammates. Back then, I wasn't the outgoing and talkative guy that I later became, so it took me several minutes to work up the nerve to approach him. When I finally did, I must have sounded like a starstruck teenager, which wasn't far from the truth considering I had only been out of high school for three years. "I'm a big fan of yours," I told Brett. "I try to imitate your hitting style." Brett smiled and nodded politely. He was probably thinking, *Good luck with that, kid.*

I also got to meet Rod Carew, who I had watched in spring training in Orlando when he played for the Minnesota Twins. Now a member of the California Angels, Carew was well on his way to his 3,000th career hit and a spot in the Hall of Fame. The whole experience overloaded my senses. There I was, wearing the white shoes that All-Stars donned back then, taking batting practice with Pete Rose and signing baseballs for fans who weren't much younger than I was. Having Andre and Gary there helped calm me down. Gary put on a show that night by belting two home runs, a performance that earned him MVP honors. Maybe the enormity of the occasion got the better of me or perhaps I was just rusty from all the time off, but when I entered the game as a pinch runner in the eighth inning, I promptly got picked off first base by Rollie Fingers. Either way, I didn't let it get to me. The night was too special to have a minor embarrassment get in the way.

After the long interruption of the season, Major League Baseball needed to win back angry fans who felt robbed of their summer entertainment. That led to a restructuring of the postseason format. Rather than just picking up where we left off with teams maintaining their existing records, the owners chose to split the season into two halves. The teams that led their divisions before the strike were declared winners of the first half of the season. In the National League East, that was the Phillies. With a clean slate, teams would compete to become second-half champions. Then, the winners of each half would square off in a best-of-five series to determine who advanced to the league championship. And if the Phillies or any other first-half winner had the best record in both halves? Then the runner-up in that division from the second half would play in the divisional series. Got that? Good, because I'm not sure I did. I just wanted to get back on the field. The '81 strike served as my first reminder that baseball is both a game and a business, a reality that would hit me over the head several more times during my career.

We hadn't played great baseball before the strike, so the chance to start from scratch in the second half of the season sounded appealing. In the previous two seasons, the division race had come down to the last weekend of the season, and the '81 season seemed destined to end the same way. We wanted to make the postseason by any means (or rules) necessary.

After a couple of near misses, Expos ownership was eager for the team to break through, and it showed a willingness to take drastic steps to get us to the top. That became clear when general manager John McHale fired manager Dick Williams less than a month before the end of the season, despite the fact that we had a winning second-half record at the time of the move.

My first reaction to the news was, "Are you serious?" I had a decent relationship with Dick, and because I didn't read the local papers or get involved in clubhouse politics, I wasn't too aware of any tension between him and my teammates or the front office. I was in a rookie fog. I didn't see or hear anything, but then again, I wasn't really looking or listening. Sometimes, however, a conversation became too loud to ignore. One thing I learned in the year that I played for Dick was that he didn't like pitchers very much. On several occasions, I remember him having a few drinks on the team plane and loudly yelling at a pitcher about this or that. Steve Rogers, who was on the receiving end of some unkind words from Dick after both retired from the game, attributed Dick's dislike for pitchers to his struggle to hit them as a player. He might have been onto something there. Dick had a decent 13-year major league career, hitting .260, but he never got past the notion that pitchers were his mortal enemy. That's likely what prompted Dick to say that he couldn't count on Steve in big games. He went a step further and called Steve a "fraud." All I can say in response to that claim is, "Wow," because I saw Steve pitch incredibly well in a lot of important contests. I just think Dick held a grudge against Steve for not pitching well in the final weeks of the '79 season, when the Expos had a chance to win the division.

As fate would have it, Steve inadvertently contributed to Dick getting let go. In a late August game against Atlanta, Dick brought Steve into the game to pinch-run at first base in the bottom of the 11th inning of a 4–4 game. With one out, Warren Cromartie hit a grounder to the first baseman, who whipped the ball over to second to start a potential double play. Steve, revved up by the rare opportunity to run the bases, attempted to disrupt shortstop Rafael Ramirez's return throw to first base by sliding into him in a way that wouldn't lead to an interference call. In the process, Steve's legs ended up on the center-field side of the bag while his left arm reached back to touch the base. The slide worked to perfection. Ramirez's throw went past the first baseman and into the dugout, enabling Cromartie to advance to second. The bad news was that Steve punctured his lung making the awkward slide, an injury that took him out of action for nearly three weeks. Afterward, Dick got second-guessed for putting his star pitcher in a situation where he could get injured.

McHale justified the firing by saying the team lacked "discipline and direction." Dick took the news like a pro, telling reporters, "If it's in the best interest of the ballclub, I understand." But I know it must have stung him to get pushed out like that. He had managed the Boston Red Sox to a pennant and the Oakland A's to two World Series championships, and he led the Expos to contender status in his five years in Montreal. I know he would have loved the opportunity to take the Expos to the postseason. Though he didn't get that chance, the managerial results he got over the course of his career earned him a deserved spot in Cooperstown in 2008.

McHale replaced Williams with Jim Fanning, a former Expos general manager who had been a part of the organization from day one. That hiring represented a weird twist to a weird season. Fanning had strong baseball credentials, but he hadn't managed at any level since the early 1960s. Suddenly, he had to step in cold and help lead a major league team to the playoffs. The upside of having Jim manage the club was that everybody knew him. He had watched a lot of us play in the minors, had negotiated many of our contracts, and had as much of a vested interest in the success of the organization as anyone around.

I probably benefited as much as anyone by having Fanning running the club. During my time on the farm, he was a constant presence. He had seen me grow as a player and had advocated for me every step of the way. Jim loved how my speed could impact a game. It genuinely excited him to see me on base. "Run, Timmy, run!" he'd yell from the stands during minor league games. He was the only guy who could call me "Timmy" and get away with it. With Jim in the dugout, even I noticed a change in atmosphere. "Gentleman Jim," as he was known, possessed all the mellowness that Dick lacked, and the team seemed looser and more relaxed after he took over.

That didn't mean that we smoothly transitioned from Dick to Jim. Panic momentarily set in after we lost the first few games under Fanning. At a players-only meeting in Chicago, pitcher Bill Lee addressed the entire team. "A lot of us wanted to see Dick go, and now he's gone," Bill said. "It's time we stop blaming the manager and take responsibility for what we do." That message resonated.

We ended up getting hot in September to overtake the St. Louis Cardinals for the division lead. Again, it all came down to the final series of the season—and I could do nothing to help my team. On September 13, in a game against the Cubs, I had fractured a bone in my right hand in a non-contact play at the plate. As I attempted to score from second base on a Dawson single, Carter motioned for me to slide into home. When I saw that the throw coming in from Cubs left fielder Jerry Morales was off line, I decided not to slide. Based on Carter's instructions, however, my brain was sending mixed signals. So I ended up doing a half-slide that looked more like a pratfall. I tried to brace myself as I tumbled toward the ground, but I still managed to land awkwardly on my hand. After the game, I called home to let my parents know what had happened. My mother and I liked to joke around with each other, so she thought I was putting her on. I assured her that I really did get hurt and walked her through the events that led to my hand getting fractured. Her response made me smile through my tears: "Next time, don't even try to slide."

Of course, an injury at such a critical time in the season is no laughing matter. Unable to swing a bat, I was limited to making pinch-running appearances for the next couple of weeks. Then, in the final week of the season, to avoid the possibility of aggravating my injury, the Expos shut me down completely. The situation reminded me of my senior year in high school when I decided not to go out for the football team but changed my mind after experiencing all the excitement at my school's season-opening game. This time, however, I wasn't getting back on the field until my injury healed.

By taking the first two games of our final series against the Mets, we clinched the second-half title and earned a postseason date with the Phillies. The first playoff berth in franchise history wasn't achieved in the traditional way, but that didn't matter to any of us. We had come very close to winning the division in 1979 and 1980, coming up short both years to teams that went on to win the World Series. We were one of the most talented teams in the game and deserved a chance to prove we could compete with the best. The Phillies, our first-round opponent, had shown in 1980 that they were the best. We had one of the youngest rosters in the league, and very few of our players had postseason experience. Almost everyone on Dallas Green's veteran team was familiar with October baseball. We had our work cut out for us.

Unfortunately, my hand injury sidelined me for the entire series. To this day, I remain disappointed that I missed out on the greatest accomplishment in Expos history, a series that included the first major league postseason game held outside of the United States. For a decade after Montreal received an expansion team in 1969, the local fans had enjoyed baseball for baseball's sake, without really paying too much attention to wins and losses. That mentality started to change in the late 1970s after the team moved from Jarry Park to Olympic Stadium, and the postseason berth in 1981 marked a real turning point in how Montrealers viewed the home team.

The Expos were no longer simply playing *against* the best teams in baseball. We had a chance to *be* the best. That so many of us came up through the Expos farm system helped create even more loyalty, both from the fan and player perspective.

We took the first two games at Olympic Stadium before the Phillies came back to win two at Veterans Stadium. That set up a decisive fifth game in Montreal that featured a match-up of aces, Steve Rogers versus Steve Carlton. Our Steve, who was no fraud that day, came out on top, throwing a six-hit shutout to send us to the National League Championship Series.

I couldn't wait to make my postseason debut. Sitting on the bench during the Phillies series felt agonizing. I wanted to play so badly that I was bouncing off the dugout walls. Finally, the day before Game 1 of the NLCS against the Dodgers, I got a clean bill of health. The Dodgers, like the Phillies, had a lot of veteran players with playoff experience. It was the third time in five years that they had reached the NLCS. Longtime Dodgers Steve Garvey, Davey Lopes, Bill Russell, Ron Cey, and Dusty Baker formed the core of the offense, and Valenzuela, Jerry Reuss, Burt Hooton, and Bob Welch comprised one of the best starting rotations in baseball. The Dodgers had crushed us during the regular season, winning five of seven games. With the pressure on, we didn't have much time to figure out a way to get the better of them in a best-of-five series.

In Game 1, at Dodger Stadium, Hooton silenced our bats. We didn't put a run on the board until the ninth inning, falling 5–1. That put the pressure squarely on our shoulders. Fortunately, our Game 2 starting pitcher, Ray Burris, stayed cool, outpitching Fernando and going the distance in a 3–0 victory. After going 1-for-4 in the series opener, I collected three hits and an RBI in Game 2.

Winning a game at Dodger Stadium rejuvenated us. In the clubhouse before Game 3, my teammates seemed relaxed and confident. Their calmness and coolness contrasted with the nervous energy I was feeling in advance of my first home playoff game. Rogers, our Game 3 starter, was on a real roll, having dominated the Phillies in two divisional series games. A member of the Expos since 1973, Steve had experienced a lot of lean times in Montreal. In the '81 postseason, I saw a determination on his face that made me realize he was going to do whatever he could to will us to victory.

The Dodgers took a 1–0 lead in the fourth inning, but that was the extent of their offensive output that night. We scored four runs in the sixth, three of them on a Jerry White home run that caused our mascot Youppi!, a big orange bear, and the sold-out Olympic Stadium crowd to go wild. Steve cruised the rest of the way, and just like that, we were one win away from the World Series.

But the Dodgers didn't give in. Through seven innings of Game 4, Hooton and Bill Gullickson matched each other pitch for pitch. A two-run home run by Garvey in the top of the eighth broke a 1–1 tie, and the Dodgers scored another four runs in the ninth to break the game open.

Having blown our first opportunity to celebrate a pennant at Olympic Stadium, we had one more chance to finish off the Dodgers. The make-or-break Game 5 was supposed to be played the following day, a Sunday, but rainy, cold weather caused a postponement until Monday afternoon.

I doubled off Fernando in the first inning and scored the first run of the game. We held onto the 1–0 lead until the fifth when Fernando helped his own cause with an RBI groundout. The score remained tied going to the ninth inning. You could feel the tension in the stadium, which unfortunately wasn't completely full because of the game taking place on a weekday afternoon.

For the second time in the series, Burris pitched extremely well. But Fanning didn't want to leave anything to chance in the ninth. That's why he summoned Rogers, and not our closer, Jeff Reardon, from the bullpen. A lot has been said and written over the years about that decision. Critics say that Fanning shouldn't have put his ace starting pitcher into such an unfamiliar situation, especially not on two days' rest. I guess it's easy with hindsight to adopt that point of view. But when Steve came out for the ninth, I know all of us had confidence that he would again get the job done. And in a situation like that one, I think it makes all the sense in the world to put your best pitcher in. And Steve was far and away our best pitcher. Steve later said the abnormal amount of adrenaline he had flowing through his veins affected his mechanics on the mound.

The inning started off well. Rogers got Garvey to weakly pop out. Cey then lifted a long fly ball to left that I caught on the warning track. That brought up Rick Monday, a tough hitter but by no means the guy in the Dodgers lineup you feared most. Monday was a left-handed hitter, so Fanning could have brought in a lefty reliever, but by this point, it was clear that he was going to stick with Rogers.

Believe me, I've given a lot of thought to that at-bat, and all these years later, I agree with Fanning's decision to let Steve face

Monday. The only thing I question is how Monday was pitched. After Steve fell behind 3-1 in the count, he didn't necessarily have to groove a fastball to Monday. The right-handed hitting Pedro Guerrero, who had struggled at the plate the entire series, was on deck. I understand that trying to get Monday to fish for a pitch outside the strike zone could have resulted in putting the go-ahead run on first base, but he was too good a fastball hitter to challenge with a pitch right down Broadway. Steve would later say that he was trying to be careful with Monday and simply missed his spot.

There's a reason that October 19, 1981, is known as "Blue Monday" in Montreal. After clubbing a towering home run to center field that gave the Dodgers a 2–1 lead, Monday threw his arms up in the air as he rounded first base. His teammates poured out onto the field to congratulate him when he crossed the plate. We still had a chance to tie or win the game in the bottom of the ninth. Valenzuela quickly got two outs before issuing back-to-back walks to Carter and Larry Parrish. We were now a hit away from likely tying the game. Tommy Lasorda pulled Fernando and called on Bob Welch to record the last out. White swung at the first pitch and bounced a ball to second base that Lopes threw to Garvey to give the Dodgers the pennant.

When the final out was recorded, Dawson, Warren Cromartie, and I, the team's Florida-born outfield trio, sat on the bench in disbelief. It was a true feeling of grief. For what seemed like an hour, I remained in the dugout, replaying the entire series in my head and wondering whether I could have done anything more to get us a different result. The answer was probably yes. I hit .238 for the series, and my speed wasn't a factor. I didn't steal a single bag and got picked off by Valenzuela in Game 2. I didn't do enough to help my team win, but in baseball, you win as a team and you lose as a team. What hurt most of all was that I thought we were better than the Dodgers. The prize awaiting us if we had won Game 5, a meeting in the World Series with the mighty Yankees, would have put an incredible spotlight on the Expos and represented a huge step forward for baseball in Canada. After one nearly full season in Montreal, I realized I was starting to think like a Canadian fan.

The disappointment of that loss to the Dodgers, who went on to beat the Yankees, grows with each passing year. With the team we had in place, it seemed like a given that we would get several more cracks at playing in the postseason. That never happened, however. My former teammates also still feel the pain. Cro talks about how at random moments during the day—when he's stopped at a red light or eating his morning cereal—he'll flash back to "Blue Monday." The loss to the Dodgers put us on the wrong side of history, but it's an event that will always bond us, not to mention all the Expos fans who had their hearts broken.

To this day, my father still laments our loss to the Dodgers, a team he was normally inclined to root for because of their courage in making Jackie Robinson the first black major league player. In 1981, however, Ned Raines Sr. was wholeheartedly rooting for his son's team. In return for his excellent work as a road grader, his employer had promised to buy him a plane ticket to Montreal for the World Series. They were even going to give him some spending money for the trip. "When Monday hit that ball out of the park, it knocked me clear out of that trip," he likes to say. The day after the game, his co-workers expressed their condolences like there had been a death in the family. And it probably looked that way, because my father was in tears.

It's open to debate whether I should have won the Rookie of the Year award in '81. I ended up losing out to Fernando in a fairly close vote. As phenomenal as Fernando pitched that season, opponents only saw him every five days. Opposing pitchers and catchers had to deal with me every day. I know one thing for sure: I would have much rather had Fernando's World Series ring than his Rookie of the Year plaque.

On the bright side, the '81 postseason helped put us on the map and brought more exposure to baseball in Montreal. More fans started showing up at events attended by Expos players. I'm not sure any of us became a bigger draw than Youppi!, whose appeal to the kids was undeniable, but during the early 1980s, I feel like I helped accomplish something that didn't seem possible a few years earlier. The pride that the *Quebecoises* felt toward their culture and language now applied to their baseball team. *Les Expos* had turned Montreal into a baseball town.

CHAPTER FOUR

4

IT'S TRUE THAT YOU CAN'T TEACH SPEED, but it's equally true that great coaches can instruct naturally fast players on how to best utilize that gift. In the minor leagues, I ran at every opportunity, and the average pitcher and catcher combo couldn't do much about it. At the major league level, I could no longer just rely on my speed. Like every other aspect of the game, stealing bases becomes more difficult in the majors. The challenge I faced when I got to Montreal was learning to get the better of pitchers with great pick-off moves and catchers with rifle arms. No one more influenced my development in this area than Expos first-base coach Steve Boros, who took a guy with raw speed and turned him into an expert on the art of the stolen base.

Steve believed in the power and mathematics of speed, not just that of runners but of pitchers and catchers as well. And he had a history of getting results. The teams he managed in the Kansas City Royals' minor league system that broke stolen-base records in the 1970s showed his methods worked. In Montreal, he always kept a stopwatch with him in the coaching box, and he would use it to measure the time it took a runner to get from first to second base, the time a pitcher took to release the ball, and the time a catcher needed to throw a ball to second base. If the sum of the second and third measurements was greater than the first, then Steve knew that a runner had a good chance of stealing a base.

By Steve's count, I needed an average of 3.2 seconds to get from first to second base. Very few pitchers and catchers could beat that time, so Steve urged me to run whenever I possibly could. His encouragement paid dividends. In my first full season in the majors, I stole 71 bases and was caught only 11 times. Seven of those unsuccessful attempts came when I broke too early and got picked off. Expos fans went wild whenever I stole a base. And it thrilled me to slide into the bag, pop back to my feet, and take in the cheers of the Olympic Stadium crowd. I gained a reputation for wearing a wide grin on my face every time I successfully swiped a bag. Not an irritating grin, but a genuine smile. I wasn't trying to rub salt in the wound of the opposition. I just couldn't contain my joy.

Steve and I shared a similar baseball philosophy. "I've always been a strong advocate of base running—not necessarily base stealing, but base running," he once told the *Los Angeles Times*. "Because ultimately, you win because you score more runs, and what I want is to be 90 feet smarter and 90 feet more aggressive than the other team. That means going to second on a short passed ball or wild pitch or from first to third on a hit to the outfield."

I couldn't say it better myself, so I won't try to. Steve was the closest thing I had to a base-running mentor. He taught me how to take leads off first base, how to time a pitcher's delivery to maximize my jump, and how to pick up on a pitcher or catcher's bad habits. He took real pleasure in watching me run, once telling reporters that he thought I had it in me to steal 150 bases in a season.

I in turn took pride in instilling fear into pitchers and catchers when I reached first base. My presence on base tended to disrupt a pitcher's rhythm. It became a game within a game. The more attention he paid to keeping me from running, the less he paid to the guy at the plate. The scoreboard operator at Olympic Stadium also did his part to get into the head of the pitcher. Whenever I or another player prompted the pitcher to throw over to first base, an image of a clucking chicken appeared on the scoreboard. If the pitcher threw over a second time, a second chicken would appear, and the clucks would grow louder. And so on and so forth. The graphic evolved over time, from a stick-figure chicken to an animated one. The fans seemed to love it, but I know the constant clucking drove some of my teammates crazy.

I'm glad I played in an era where teams understood the value of base running. Nowadays, speedy hitters tend to put the brakes on when they reach base, because they don't want to get thrown out with a slugger at the plate. You hear a lot about the death of the stolen base, especially when players like Billy Hamilton of the Cincinnati Reds come along, reminding everyone that running can still be an important part of the game. The numbers speak for themselves, however. In 1983, every National League team except the Chicago Cubs stole at least 100 bases, In 2015, National League teams averaged 88 stolen bases, two fewer than I stole by myself in 1983. It's not that players back then were faster than they are today. The opposite is probably true. It's that the game itself has fundamentally changed. Part of the decline had to do with the rise of performance-enhancing drugs in the 1990s. With balls flying out of stadiums at an unprecedented rate, no team wanted to risk making outs on the base paths. In the steroid era, the concept of "small ball" fell by the wayside. Even in the post-steroid era, however, it's rare to see a player steal more than 50 bases in a season.

Boros played a major role in my education as a player. He taught me how to use my legs to help us win games. Other coaches helped me with my fielding and hitting. During my rookie year, my body did everything I wanted it to. In addition to stealing 71 bases in 88 games, I hit .304. But as I mentioned earlier, my mental and emotional development lagged behind my physical advancements. That's what led me to become involved with drugs in 1982. I am grateful that I got the help I needed and that the Expos organization stood by me during this difficult period in my life.

I didn't realize it until years later, but some of the people who watched me play every day in 1982 realized I had a problem. Expos broadcaster Dave Van Horne talks about the time I drew a walk in Atlanta, and instead of tossing the bat toward our dugout and jogging to first base, I dropped my bat at the plate and started wandering toward the Braves dugout. This incident occurred at a time when I was mired in a terrible batting slump. The shouts of my teammates pierced my haze and I embarrassedly went down to first base. After the game, Van Horne took Expos general manager John McHale aside to ask him what was going on with me. "John, I've held back on criticizing Raines on air, but his performance and his behavior is hurting this team badly right now," he said. As soon as Dave finished his sentence, McHale jumped in to request a favor: "Dave, I'm asking that you remain supportive of Tim. We have an issue that we have to work out. Just give it some time."

Except for occasional lapses when I drew attention to myself, I maintained appearances pretty well. My drug problem caused me to miss only one game, and I put up All-Star caliber numbers in 1982. But if I had fallen any deeper into drugs, my performance would have started to suffer. That's why it was so important to nip the problem in the bud. I'm not sure I would have rebounded the way I did without the support and friendship of my teammate, Andre Dawson. He stayed by my side every step of the way and made sure I never came close to relapsing.

Thank god for Andre. That's all I can say. Without him, I honestly don't know what might have happened to me. From the moment he burst on the scene in 1977, he gained admirers all over baseball. I was in my first year in the minors when Andre won the Rookie of the Year award. Before I ever really got to know him, I looked at him as a role model, another Florida guy from a big family, who took the major leagues by storm despite not being a top draft pick. As our respective careers flourished, my admiration for him only grew. It seemed like he was having his knees operated on every season, but he played through the pain. I can't remember ever hearing him complain about his knees or make excuses. He showed up at the ballpark early to soak in the clubhouse whirlpool, wrap his knees, and meet with the team trainer. Then he went out and conducted his business in the most professional way imaginable.

I looked up to Andre in every way, both literally and figuratively. He had a slugger's physique and a gentleman's temperament. He was the best player I had ever seen and I wanted to emulate him in every way. Andre has always been a perceptive guy, and he picked up on the fact that something was off with me in 1982. He would later tell me that he thought about stepping in and asking if he could help me in any way, but he chose instead to respect my privacy. In the end, I didn't go to him asking for help, nor did he attempt to perform any kind of intervention with me. We just kind of came together naturally. The *Montreal Gazette* had already revealed everything about my drug problem, so there was no need for me to rehash that with Andre. Instead, at spring training in 1983, we talked baseball. I told him I wanted to be a player like him and hoped to earn the type of respect he commanded. "I need you to show me the way," I told him.

The more time I spent with Andre, the more my true personality started to come out. In my first seasons in the majors, I felt obligated to conduct myself in a serious manner all the time. I thought that having fun would make me come across as less of a professional. I observed Andre, and it didn't look like he was having much fun, so why should I try to be any different? At the ballpark, I hid behind a figurative curtain, repressing my true instincts to laugh it up and have a good time. Away from the park, of course, I indulged too much in a good-time lifestyle.

My friendship with Andre had mutual benefits. As I became a more fun-loving type of guy, Andre started coming out of his shell, too. He was one of the biggest and strongest guys in the game. No one ever messed with him...except for me. During batting practice I'd spar with him, realizing that his size, quick hands, and massive wingspan made it impossible for me to land any jabs with my glove. In the clubhouse, we'd go another round, wrapping our hands in sanitary socks to soften the blows. Sometimes I'd come up from behind him and mount an attack. Then I'd take off running.

I realized that if Andre Dawson could put up with my antics, then anyone could. We anchored the Expos outfield together and shared a lot of laughs away from the ballpark. I'll always remember the time Andre, Warren Cromartie, and I were out at a Montreal restaurant when a man approached Andre, barely able to speak he was so starstruck. Andre smiled at him, clearly flattered that his presence could put someone in such a state. Keep in mind that back in the day, Andre sported Jheri curls like a certain pop star known for a string of hit singles and his earlier work with The Commodores. Finally, the man calmed down and managed to put a sentence together. "Oh my goodness," he said, "my friends back home will never believe I met you! I love your music so much, Mr. Richie."

When Virginia gave birth to our second son in July 1983, we had an easy time selecting a name: Andre. We wanted to honor my friend and all he had done to help get me on the straight and narrow. My second son even took on a miniature version of his godfather's nickname: Little Hawk. My mom came up from Florida a few weeks before Andre's birth to help out around the house and look after Tim Jr. Compared to a year earlier, I was a different man, seeing the world through clear eyes. The support of my mom, my wife, the rest of my family, and Hawk got me through that tough period and prepared me for every challenge that stood ahead. It choked me up when Hawk mentioned me during his Hall of Fame induction speech in 2010, saying that I was like a brother to him. That feeling is mutual.

After getting clean, I embraced a quiet and sober existence. Rather than staying out all night, hitting up all the hot spots in town, I went back to my apartment after games and immediately crawled into bed. My wife and I started spending more time together with our sons.

I did develop another addiction around this time, but one that was much safer. The habit dated back to my childhood, actually, when I'd sit with my mom as she watched the various soap operas that aired on weekday mornings and afternoons. Her favorites were *All My Children* and *Another World*. I was just a kid, so I didn't really appreciate all of the craziness that was unfolding on the television screen. I just remember that a lot of people got stabbed in the back, sometimes literally. My mom turned watching soaps into a participation sport by yelling at the screen when characters did something particularly cruel, stupid, or selfish.

In the comfort of my Montreal apartment, I rediscovered the joy of soaps. Most days, I'd sleep in until about 10:00 AM, and between then and the time I had to report to the ballpark, I'd binge on the daytime dramas. Their plot lines were totally unrealistic, but no more so than the so-called reality shows you see everywhere today. *General Hospital* became my favorite. This was many, many years before DVRs, so I made sure I was in front of the TV to keep up with what was going on in Port Charles, particularly if it had to do with the show's most popular characters, Luke and Laura. The couple had already gotten married by that time, but their wedding vows didn't bring stability to their lives. Soon after tying the knot, Laura got kidnapped and was left for dead. But was she *really* dead? The show never failed to leave you in suspense. That's how it hooked you. And I took the bait. I came to respect the actors and actresses who starred in the soaps. They did an unbelievable number of shows per year and always had to show up prepared to do a scene. In that way, they weren't that much different than baseball players.

Compared to my wild antics of a year earlier, my new lifestyle might have seemed boring. But I was okay with that. I didn't want to be around drugs or drug users anymore. I didn't even want to be in places where people smoked cigarettes, which meant I couldn't frequent most restaurants in Montreal. I learned at an early age that I didn't like cigarettes and couldn't figure out why most of the adult population of Montreal seemed to be puffing on them.

Hawk, Cro, and I formed a pretty good team. When Cro first laid eyes on me in 1979, he wondered what I was doing on a baseball field. "Shouldn't you be lined up in the I-formation in somebody's backfield, homey?" he joked. The irony of having an outfield comprised entirely of Floridians in chilly Montreal wasn't lost on us. We got nicknamed the "I-95 outfield," but amongst ourselves, we called each other "homey." In a nod toward our friendship, Cro named a radio show he later hosted in Miami, "Call Me Homey." Cro liked to run his mouth, in a good way. I sat back and enjoyed his antics. Andre played the role of the straight man with his permanent scowl, immaculate locker, and shirts buttoned all the way to the top.

In some ways, Cro became the voice of the team. A veteran Expo, he started his professional career a few hours up the road from Montreal in Quebec City. On long minor league bus trips that took him past the lights of Montreal, he'd dream of being a part of the city. Cro embraced Canadian culture. He married a woman from Quebec and always spoke highly of his adopted homeland. The man had a way with words, which made him popular among reporters. And Canada returned the love. The rock group Rush, one of Canada's biggest bands of all time, befriended Cro and even paid homage to him on one of their album covers. Every team needs a goodwill ambassador and Cro was ours.

There were no shortage of role models in the Expos clubhouse. Gary Carter had a huge influence on how I played the game. The two things I remember most about him were his work ethic and the smile always plastered on his face. I considered him the ultimate professional. Gary really came into his own in 1980, finishing second in National League MVP voting to Mike Schmidt of the Phillies. He played with a swagger that his teammates embraced and his opponents hated. I saw him from both sides of the ledger. If I didn't know him as well as I did, I probably wouldn't have cared for him during his later years with the New York Mets. But his cockiness didn't bother me. His nickname fit him to a tee. He was "The Kid," and his child-like joy for the game never dimmed.

Gary, more than Andre or anybody else in the clubhouse, relished the role of team leader. Gary's outspokenness and fondness for the television cameras contrasted with Andre's strong but silent personality. In postgame interviews, Andre would give short and direct answers to questions from the media. I'm sure the reporters much preferred the dialogues with Cro and Gary, who could go on at length about the particulars of a game, their own performances, or anything else on a journalist's mind. Gary also loved to ham it up in TV commercials. One in particular that I remember, for

7-Up, featured Gary getting bowled over by a pitch from his young daughter, Christy.

While Andre chose to lead by example, Gary tried to influence his teammates with both words and actions. As both players emerged into stars, a professional rivalry developed between them. They butted heads at times, but I have no doubt that their status as co-leaders in the clubhouse helped make each of them, and all of us, better.

It was a terrible loss for the Expos family and the baseball community when Gary died of brain cancer in 2012. As I said at his funeral, you almost felt guilty if you weren't happy when Gary was around. He had the kind of infectious personality that made you view the world with a positive attitude.

Al Oliver was another teammate I looked up to. Al was a 13-year major league veteran when he came to Montreal from Texas right before the start of the 1982 season. While I was struggling to keep up appearances at the ballpark every day, Al turned in the best season of his career, leading the National League in hits, doubles, RBIs, batting average, and total bases. Like Andre and Gary, Al had a very businesslike approach to the game. Nobody squared up a pitch and hit a ball harder than Al.

A lot of writers over the years mused about my Hall of Fame candidacy. I feel fortunate to have remained on the ballot for 10 years and to have had so many people advocating for my entry into Cooperstown. Now that it's finally happened, I can't help but think about players like Al who didn't get a fair shot at enshrinement. Despite more than 2,700 career hits and a lifetime batting average of .303, Al appeared on the Hall of Fame ballot just one time. He was removed from consideration after getting just 4.3 percent of the vote in 1991. I'm a prime example of a player whose candidacy was aided by a decade's worth of debate and discussion. I feel like Al would have had a fighting chance at reaching Cooperstown if writers had more time to examine his body of work.

I felt honored to join my teammates at the 1982 All-Star Game, which was played in front of our home fans at Olympic Stadium. Steve Rogers won the game, and Al, Gary, and Andre all got hits in the National League's 4–1 win. I went hitless but managed to steal a base. A lot of the '82 season is a blur to me, but that night stands out very clearly in my memory.

I got my life and career back on track during the 1983 season. My first priority was getting clean. And once I accomplished that, I set another goal: helping the Expos win a championship. Despite falling to third place in the National League East in '82, I felt we had all the pieces to get to the World Series in the coming years. The core of our team remained largely intact, and the addition of Al and the emergence of Jeff Reardon as an elite closer seemed to give us the last little push we needed.

The front office grew frustrated with our perennial bridesmaid status. Jim Fanning resigned as manager on the final day of the 1982 season, and the Expos brought in veteran skipper Bill Virdon, who had led the Pirates and Astros to division titles, to replace him. We had been expected to win the NL East in '82 but fell well short of that goal. That didn't prevent a lot of baseball writers from picking us to win the division again the next season.

Unfortunately, nothing went as planned in '83. Despite a lack of consistency throughout the summer, we stood in first place in the

National League East on September 13. Then we fell flat on our faces, losing both games of a doubleheader to the Phillies, a team of aging veterans that caught fire and ran away with the division title. In three short weeks, we went from leading the division by half a game to trailing Philadelphia by eight games.

In late September 1983, I became the first player since Ty Cobb to steal 70 bases and knock in 70 runs in a season. That was all well and good, but my personal accomplishments didn't mean a whole lot if we didn't win as a team. Based on my growing reputation as a premier base stealer, Jim Wohlford, a reserve outfielder, tried to coin a new nickname for me: Roadrunner. Whenever he saw me, he'd laugh and say, "Roadrunner. Meep! Meep!" Despite Jim's best efforts, I remained "Rock."

I didn't know it at the time, but looking back, it's pretty clear to see that our window for success, which had been wide open for five seasons, started to close after the '83 season. Cro left to play in Japan. Al got traded to the Giants to make room at first base for the newest Expo, Pete Rose, who signed a one-year contract with the club. We just didn't feel like the same cohesive unit that we were when I first came to the majors. But I believed we still had enough talent to get over the top.

A lot of people don't remember that Pete played in Montreal. That's understandable, because if you blinked, you easily could have missed his time with us. At the start of the 1984 season, he was closing in on 43 years of age and his 4,000th career major league hit. He came from a Phillies team that had won the pennant in 1983 and a World Series in 1980. And his successes with the Big Red Machine were legendary. McHale obviously hoped that Pete's competitive spirit and winning ways would rub off on us. "We seem to have lacked some of the qualities Pete has," McHale told *The New York Times* during spring training.

It also made sense from a business standpoint. Fans wanted to see Pete in action as he chased Ty Cobb's all-time hit record. The Expos even agreed to pay him a bonus if the team reached certain attendance benchmarks during the season.

In Pete, we were getting a legend. The guy knew more about baseball than anyone I had ever been around. He talked about the finer points of the game in the clubhouse, the team plane, and anywhere else he might corner you. I didn't know if having him on the roster would make us a better team, but I did resolve to learn as much from him as I could. Pete went out of his way to let people know that he appreciated me and my game. "Rock can beat you in more ways than any other player in the league," he said in *Sports Illustrated*. That obviously made me feel good.

To accommodate Pete, who had collected most of his hits from the leadoff spot, Virdon moved me to third in the lineup. Some players may have pushed back at the idea of being removed from a role at which they had excelled. I didn't see things that way, however. I embraced the switch and viewed it as a welcome challenge to hit in the middle of the lineup. In previous seasons, I had demonstrated my ability to get on base and use my speed to help the team. But I considered myself a complete player, not just a Punch-and-Judy hitter who poked singles. In the three hole, I had an opportunity to show that I could drive in runs as well as score them.

That wasn't the only change I experienced that season. Hawk's knees had taken such a pounding in his seven seasons on the hard

Olympic Stadium turf that the Expos decided it would be in his and the team's best interests to move him from center field to right field, where he would have to do less running. So, in 1984, I became the Expos' everyday center fielder.

I viewed the position switch as a positive development, too. During my rookie season, I had successfully transitioned from second base to left field to fill a void in the outfield. Over the next few seasons, I played the infield from time to time whenever our everyday second baseman was injured. But with the exception of one game in 1983, I had never before played center field. Andre had dibs on the position, and no one played it better than him. But from a physical standpoint, it made sense for him to move over to right. I didn't have a rocket arm or the height to climb walls and rob home runs, but I definitely had the speed to track down balls. I liked how all the action played out in front of me when I stood in center. If I misjudged a ball as it came off the bat, I usually had enough time to regroup and make up for my mistake. If the ball stayed in the park, I felt like I had a good chance to get to it. Having Andre beside me helped a lot. Without encroaching on my territory, he maintained his leadership role in the outfield. There's no question, he helped make me better during my only season in center.

Four of the first five hitters to come to the plate for us on opening day (Pete, myself, Andre, and Gary Carter) ended up with Hall of Fame caliber numbers. On paper, we looked like we could do some damage. When all was said and done, however, we ended up with the second-lowest run total in the National League. Our pitching helped keep us in a lot of games, but not enough to remain competitive. We finished the season in fifth place with a 78–83 record, our first losing year since 1978.

Pete got his 4,000[th] hit in mid-April. By mid-August, he was gone, traded to the Reds. A couple of weeks later, our manager exited, too. At the end of the '82 season, McHale had replaced Fanning with Virdon. Two years later, he replaced Virdon with Fanning. It was one of McHale's last actions as general manager. He resigned that position near the end of the '84 season but remained on as team president.

Major on-the-field changes followed, most significantly with the trade of Gary Carter to the Mets. In what was considered one of the biggest blockbuster deals of the era, Gary went to New York in return for four young players, including shortstop Hubie Brooks. From the Expos' standpoint, Gary's value had pretty much hit an all-time high, and the team felt moving him would help it rebuild. Despite our offensive struggles in 1984, Gary led the National League in RBIs, while hitting a career-high .294. An Expo for 11 seasons, Gary could have vetoed the trade based on his years of service with the team, but the chance to go to a team on the rise proved too good to pass up. I admire the fact that despite his later successes in New York that Gary opted to become the first player enshrined in Cooperstown as a member of the Expos.

I knew enough about the makeup of successful ballclubs to know that the Carter trade wouldn't be good for our record. Until that deal, I felt we had been moving in a positive direction as an organization and remained just a player or two away from going all the way. The Carter trade represented a step backward. The Big Three of Carter, Dawson, and Raines had been reduced to the Big Two. You never know how a shakeup in personnel will affect a team, but deep down I realized that, without The Kid, our chances of bringing a World Series to Montreal had suffered a major blow.

CHAPTER FIVE

5

DURING SPRING TRAINING IN 1985, my past drug use again became a topic of discussion when I testified before a federal grand jury in Pittsburgh investigating cocaine use in Major League Baseball.

My public battle with the drug in 1982 made me an obvious candidate to appear in front of the grand jury, so it didn't really surprise me when I received my subpoena in the mail. I didn't mind telling my story again. After all, I had done so already in much more public forums, first in the pages of the *Montreal Gazette* and then in *Sports Illustrated* and other publications. But it's one thing to talk to a newspaper or magazine about your own experiences and another entirely to testify in a formal court setting under oath about the who, what, when, where, and why of those experiences.

Unlike hearings and trials in open court, grand juries conduct secret proceedings that determine whether enough evidence exists to proceed further against the target or targets of an investigation, in this case the dealers deemed responsible for providing cocaine and other drugs to major league ballplayers. The promise of juicy details about players' drug use caused reporters from around the country to flock to the courthouse during grand jury proceedings, and later that year, for the trial itself.

On the March day that I testified before the grand jury, I left the courthouse without giving a comment to the press. My attorney told reporters, "He has no comment. He doesn't even want to acknowledge he's Tim Raines." My involvement with the drug trials began and ended with my grand jury testimony. I wasn't one of the six current players to receive immunity to testify at the trial itself, which resulted in the convictions of seven men. My name did surface at the trial, however, when John Milner, a former teammate of mine in Montreal, testified that he, Expos outfielder Rowland Office, and I snorted coke together. I won't deny that that happened. Based on what came out at the trial, Major League Baseball fined about a dozen players and ordered them to perform community service. I was among a handful of players—and the only Expo—who the league required to submit to random drug testing for an indefinite period of time. I had no problem with that punishment because I had nothing to hide.

I can't help but wonder what might have happened in 1982 if some of my teammates and I hadn't gotten consumed with drugs. On the eve of the drug trials, Expos president John McHale had the following to say on the subject: "I don't think there's any doubt in '82 that that whole scenario cost us a chance to win…When we all woke up to what was going on, we found there were at least eight players on our club who were into this thing."

It's difficult to say whether the Expos were any different than other teams of that era when it came to drug use. Certainly a lot has come out about the extracurricular activities of players all over the league to suggest that the problem had more to do with the time than the place. It was simply a part of society back then. Was it the reason we didn't win the division in '82? Probably not. But I'll be the first to admit that it may have been a negative contributing factor.

With my testimony in Pittsburgh, I felt like I had once and for all put the past behind me. Coming off my fourth straight All-Star season, I was looking forward to seeing whether our retooled team could become competitive.

Prior to the 1985 season, I went to salary arbitration. The Expos were offering me a cool mil. My agent, Tom Reich, and I believed I was worth $1.2 million. An arbitrator in Chicago ruled in my favor, making me the recipient of the largest amount of money in an arbitration case at the time.

The 1985 season represented the start of the Buck Rodgers era in Montreal. Ever since Dick Williams was fired near the end of the '81 season, we had lacked a consistent voice calling the shots in the dugout. In what should have been the golden years of the franchise, we alternated between Jim Fanning and Bill Virdon, with neither manager able to harness the talent the team clearly possessed. That's not a knock on Jim or Bill. At the end of the day, it's the responsibility of the players to take the field and get the job done.

The '85 season also marked the end of Steve Rogers' great career in Montreal. For nearly a decade, Steve was our ace and one of the best pitchers in the National League. Our playoff run during the strike-shortened season wouldn't have been possible without him. A shoulder injury in '84 reduced Steve to a shadow of his former self, and his streak of seven straight double-digit-winning seasons came to an abrupt end when he finished with a 6–15 record '85. In May, the Expos released him.

All things considered, we put together a pretty good year in 1985. We won 84 games and lost 77. There were definite bright spots. In Rogers' absence, Bryn Smith stepped in and gave us a top-of-the-line starting pitcher, winning 18 games on the strength of a nasty curveball that National League hitters just couldn't figure out. "Pretty good" might get you a wild-card spot nowadays, but at a time when only division winners advanced to the playoffs, it didn't get us anywhere close to the postseason.

Back in left field and in the leadoff spot on a permanent basis, I hit .320 and made another All-Star team. I also stole 70 bases, the second most in the National League. If you had told me before the season that the league leader would steal 110 bases, I would have said you were crazy. But that's the number that Vince Coleman of the St. Louis Cardinals swiped in his rookie year. That Cardinals team, which featured two 20-game winners and five players who stole 30 or more bases, was a testimony to what pitching, speed, and defense can do for a club. How adept were Coleman and Willie McGee, who hit second in the lineup, at reaching base and scoring runs? Tom Herr, who normally batted third, knocked in 110 runs that season, more than doubling his total from the season before. And he eclipsed the 100-RBI mark despite only hitting eight home runs. The Cardinals won 101 games and the pennant before falling in the World Series to the Kansas City Royals.

Baseball is funny. When I broke into the majors, the Phillies and Pirates ruled the National League East. By the middle of the 1980s, the balance of power completely shifted. Philadelphia and

Pittsburgh had become also-rans, while the Cardinals and New York Mets had turned into powerhouses. Where did that leave us? Somewhere in the middle, a place we would stay for the rest of my time in Montreal.

In 1986, it was the Mets' turn to electrify the baseball world. Riding the arms of Dwight Gooden, Ron Darling, Bob Ojeda, and Sid Fernandez, and the bats of Keith Hernandez, Gary Carter, and Darryl Strawberry, the Mets left every other NL East team in the dust, winning 108 games in the regular season. We played solid baseball in the first half of the season, but there was just no way to keep pace with the Mets. They were a special team, the perfect combination of young and veteran players. They had swagger and flair, too. They came to town, partied into the wee hours, and then went out and kicked your butt the next day. I had grown up thinking of the Mets as loveable losers. The '86 team ended that.

I remember seeing Strawberry when he exploded on the scene in 1983 and thinking he had what it took to be the best player who ever played the game. He remained one of my favorite players to watch over the next several seasons. It eventually came out that Straw was battling some of the same demons that I faced during my early years in the big leagues. He ended up having a very successful major league career, but I can't help but wonder how dominant he might have been if he had gotten his personal issues under control. The same goes for Gooden.

The Mets finished off their incredible season by beating the Boston Red Sox in the World Series. I badly wanted the opportunity to play deep into October, but every fall I found myself back at home in Florida watching other guys compete. With the Mets,

Gary finally got to fulfill a dream of celebrating a championship. He played a pivotal role against Boston, hitting two home runs in Game 4 of the series. I didn't feel envy toward Gary. I was genuinely happy for him. All I could hope was that my time would come.

As my team tried to figure things out, I continued to put up impressive individual numbers. I led the National League with a .334 batting average in 1986, an achievement made possible by working on my bunting skills during the off-season. I also became the first player in major league history to steal 70 or more bases in six consecutive seasons. By this point in my career, I had learned to fully trust my instincts on the base paths. I didn't need a first- or third-base coach to tell me when to run. That's exactly what my base-running mentor, Steve Boros, hoped would eventually happen. A person who's afraid to take chances isn't going to realize his full potential. That's true on the baseball field and in every walk of life.

In '86, Peter Gammons of *Sports Illustrated* proclaimed Rickey Henderson and me the best leadoff men ever to play the game. Rickey had three seasons of 100 or more steals to his name, and as the article noted, he wore a gold medallion around his neck etched with "130," the record number of steals he had in 1982. As far as I was concerned, Rickey and I always had a friendly relationship. We played most of our careers in different leagues, so we never developed the type of rivalry that we might have if our teams had competed head to head on a regular basis. I always admired Rickey. He and I had similar instincts that were undoubtedly shaped by our respective backgrounds on the football field. I had been offered an opportunity to play running back at the University of Florida, and

Rickey had been recruited by a slew of Division I football programs looking for the next O.J. Simpson.

Rickey and I possessed the same tools and approach to the game, but our personalities couldn't have been more different. I liked to put on a good show, but I never considered myself a showman. Rickey, on the other hand, proudly wore that label. Whether he was celebrating home runs or stealing bases with the outcome of a game already decided, Rickey wanted the world to know that he was the greatest. On the day in May 1991 when Rickey broke Lou Brock's record for career stolen bases, he pulled the base out of the ground, grabbed a microphone, and proclaimed to the crowd at the Oakland Coliseum, "Lou Brock was the symbol of great base stealing, but today I am the greatest of all time. Thank you." Never had so much been said in so few words. But that was Rickey.

I never looked at my statistics and compared myself to others. Every stolen base I attempted was to help my team win games, not to pad my stats. I heard it said time and again that I was "the Rickey Henderson of the National League." That didn't bother me. Rickey was an outstanding player. But maybe he was "the Tim Raines of the American League."

I never tried to compete with Rickey. That would have been futile. I ultimately came to the conclusion that Rickey and I stole bases for different reasons. In my opinion, Rickey stole bases for Rickey, and I hope that doesn't sound negative. Rickey believed he was the greatest of all time and he sought to back that assertion up with cold, hard stats. I didn't resent him for that, but at the same time, I made a conscious decision never to play the game that way. On the few occasions when I got to spend time with Rickey, we enjoyed each other's company, having fun and cracking jokes. I honestly don't know how he truly felt about me, but I can say for sure that I respected his talent and liked him as a person.

When I became a free agent after the '86 season, my track record should have put me in a position to sign for big money with any number of teams. But that's not what happened, because the owners teamed up and decided to pass on signing players from other teams, forcing them to stay with their current teams. In 1988, an arbitrator ruled that baseball owners had acted "in concert" to prevent free agents like myself from signing with other clubs. It was a practice known as collusion. Our Collective Bargaining Agreement stated that "Players shall not act in concert with other Players and Clubs shall not act in concert with other Clubs." In the words of Donald Fehr, then the executive director of the Major League Players Association, "the owners got together and rigged the game."

Dating back to the strike of '81, I didn't have a real understanding of the behind-the-scenes business dealings that seemed to have become as much a part of the game as home runs and strikeouts. The situation in '81 didn't feel personal. The one five years later very much did. My first clue that the owners had rigged the system came shortly after the end of the '86 season when Expos management basically made me a contract offer in the local paper. It didn't seem right for them to publicize the terms of a would-be contract without negotiating with my agent and me behind closed doors. That definitely got the process off on the wrong foot. But it only got worse from there. After we entered into talks with the Expos, we noticed a trend. Every time my agent and I turned down a proposed deal, the Expos would counter with an offer of even less money. "These guys aren't fighting fair," Tom said in disgust after one of those meetings.

Baseball in Montreal had arrived at a crossroads. In 1986, we drew just over 1.1 million fans to the ballpark, fewer than half as many who came out to see us in 1983. Team ownership clearly had an eye on the bottom line, but in my mind, that didn't give them the right to take advantage of players, especially ones who had contributed so much to the team. I felt loyalty toward the Expos and wanted to continue my career in Montreal, but I also needed to stand up for myself and all of the other players who found themselves in a similar situation. "The dollar figure isn't everything," I said at the time. "The club I would love to sign with is the one I feel is going to win. That doesn't rule out Montreal, though…We've had a good relationship and I would certainly play there again if things work out."

It didn't appear things would work out, however. The Expos' top offer was a three-year, $4.8 million deal. That came out to an annual raise of only about $100,000. The Expos were also trying to shortchange my teammate and friend Andre Dawson. He too held out in the hopes that another team would sign him.

I considered it my right to test the free-agency waters, so in November 1986, that's exactly what I did, a move that put me on the open market and eligible to sign with the highest bidder. Surely, I thought, there were teams out there who would love to sign a player with my skill set.

The Houston Astros called to offer me a contract that wasn't worth nearly as much as I was already making. The Atlanta Braves and Seattle Mariners showed some interest but not enough to make a formal offer. Padres manager Larry Bowa made it known through the media that he wanted me in a San Diego uniform, but Padres ownership didn't have the will to make it happen. They turned down our proposal of a one-year, $1.3 million contract that included incentive clauses. The Los Angeles Dodgers, who were near the top of my list of preferred teams, didn't chime in at all.

As Tom waited to field a serious offer, the January deadline by which free agents could re-sign with their current teams came and went, leaving Andre and me ineligible to negotiate with the Expos again until May 1. The team didn't seem to mind. If we played for the Expos in '87, that was fine. If not, that seemed to be fine with them, too. That put us in no man's land. Other star players found themselves in the same kind of limbo. When the January re-signing date passed, eight unsigned free agents remained: me, Andre, Ron Guidry, Lance Parrish, Rich Gedman, Bob Horner, Bob Boone, and Doyle Alexander.

The owners' unwillingness to pay the best players in the game what we deserved left a bad taste in my mouth. Baseball fans should have been talking about my accomplishments on the field, not my contract situation. All I wanted was to play ball. But I also felt I deserved fair compensation for my services. It didn't seem right that a bunch of rich owners could get together and collude to drive salaries down. It became a matter of principle.

At this point in the process, Andre took a drastic step and went to Chicago Cubs general manager Dallas Green with a blank contract, instructing Green to put down whatever sum of money he saw fit. Intrigued, the Cubs ended up signing Andre for $500,000, plus incentives, a lot less than he would have earned with the

Expos. But it made sense for Andre to take a deal that allowed him to continue his career on his own terms—and away from the hard artificial turf at Olympic Stadium. He figured he could demonstrate his true worth by having a strong first season in Chicago.

Parrish, a six-time All-Star with the Detroit Tigers, was the only other of the unsigned free agents to go to a different team. He signed a contract with the Philadelphia Phillies for about the same amount he had earned in Detroit.

I went nowhere. As the rules dictated, I missed spring training and the first month of the '87 season. Back home in Florida, I kept myself in shape by working out with a high school team in Sarasota. On May 1, I checked back in with the Expos, who chose to put an end to the game of chicken by sweetening the contract offer a little bit. I signed on the dotted line.

I was hardly in game shape, but after getting four hits in a practice game at our spring training facility, I was told to join the Expos for a weekend series at Shea Stadium against the world champion Mets. The Saturday game happened to be NBC's Game of the Week, a rare opportunity for the Expos to play in front of a national audience.

Even a reigning batting champion needs to keep his skills sharp. I hadn't faced major league pitching since the end of the previous season, making the routine seem unfamiliar. I felt like I was trapped in the middle of an anxiety dream in which you show up for work horribly unprepared to do your job. During batting practice, some of my teammates gathered around the cage to watch me take cuts, but I couldn't seem to hit anything out of the infield. I felt really embarrassed, not to mention completely disoriented. I had never faced the pitcher going for the Mets that day, rookie David Cone. And for the first time in my career, I didn't see Hawk in the clubhouse. His absence in the cleanup spot meant I would hit third in front of Tim Wallach and be responsible for driving in more runs. It felt like a new era had begun that I wasn't quite prepared for.

The four hours that followed helped calm my nerves and set the tone for one of the most successful seasons of my career. In my first at-bat, I swung at Cone's first pitch and hit a triple off the right-field wall. In the third inning, I stole my first base of the season. After picking up two more hits, I could feel the rust falling off onto the Shea Stadium grass. In the top of the 10th inning of a 6–6 game, I came to the plate with the bases loaded against Mets reliever Jesse Orosco, a pitcher who really had my number. Not on this day, however. Batting from the right side, I took Orosco's second pitch, a fastball, over the left-field wall for a game-winning grand slam. Those watching at home heard NBC broadcasters Vin Scully and Joe Garagiola go wild. My teammates swarmed me. Some of them even bowed down to me in mock reverence. The Mets players watched me cross home plate with a combination of scorn and admiration. New York second baseman Wally Backman later told *The New York Times*, "That was an incredible thing we just saw." Longtime Expos broadcaster Dave Van Horne called it one of the most exciting single performances he witnessed in his 32 years calling Expos games.

That game remains one of the most memorable of my career. In addition to solidifying my role as a team leader, it served as a great national showcase for the Expos. I think it also showed that teams had made a mistake by not bidding for my services.

The rest of the 1987 season had a different feel for me, mostly because Hawk wasn't around. Of all the relationships I developed during my playing days, none had a stronger foundation than my friendship with Andre. Because we both were free agents, I knew we would likely go in different directions, but I held out hope that we might somehow end up playing for the same team. As it turned out, Andre's decision to sign the blank contract with the Cubs went down as one of the most brilliant decisions in baseball history. In his first season in Chicago, he hit a career-high 49 home runs, and despite the Cubs' last-place finish in the National League East, he took home the National League MVP award. In Montreal, Andre had flown under the radar somewhat. There's no question that playing north of the border cost players like us the exposure we would have received in a major American city. Thanks to the WGN Superstation in Chicago, Andre got the opportunity to show off his skills to a much wider audience. The 1987 season established him as a national superstar and a hero to Cubs fans.

At that year's All-Star Game in Oakland, I entered the game as a defensive replacement in the bottom of the sixth inning expecting to get maybe one at-bat late in the game. It was my seventh appearance in the Midsummer Classic, and I had yet to get a hit in any of them. In the ninth inning of a 0–0 game, I broke that streak by lining a one-out single up the middle off Dave Righetti. The game ended up going into extra innings, which gave me another opportunity to come to the plate. In the top of the 11th, I singled off Tom Henke. After all those hitless years, I was finally starting to get the hang of this All-Star thing. Neither team broke through with a run, so I came up yet again in the 13th inning, this time with two runners on base. Jay Howell of the A's threw a pitch I liked, and I lined it in the gap for a two-run triple. My three-hit performance earned me MVP honors, an extra-special honor considering it turned out to be the last All-Star Game I would ever play in.

In the games that actually counted in 1987, I also excelled. Despite missing the first month of the season, I finished with a career-high 18 home runs and a .330 batting average. My run of six straight seasons with 70 or more stolen bases ended, but I still managed to swipe 50 while getting caught only five times. For leading us to a 91-win record, Buck Rodgers walked away with the National League Manager of the Year award.

I don't think anybody expected the retooled Expos to play as well as we did in 1987, most certainly not the many baseball writers who predicted a last-placc finish. When I joined the team in early May, our record stood at 8–13, and it looked like the experts had it right. Then something pretty incredible happened. Our patchwork team of mid-career players put together a run that kept us within reach of the Cardinals and Mets all season. Unfortunately, our 91 wins were only good enough for third place.

Who knows what might have happened if I had been in uniform all season. That question obviously can't be answered, and the fact that it can even be asked is a sad commentary on what happened to me and other players who had to beg teams to sign them or sit out part of the season because of collusion. It goes without saying that Andre's departure left a huge void in the middle of our lineup. Even an average season by his standards would have resulted in the Expos finishing with a couple of extra wins. In his place, we employed a platoon in center field of Herm Winningham and Reid Nichols.

Things being what they were, I had no choice but to look ahead. And 1987 provided some hope that maybe the Expos would somehow find a way to stay competitive. Wallach, one of the steadiest fielding and hitting third basemen in the league, turned his game up a couple notches, reaching career highs in batting average and RBIs, a performance that earned him a fourth-place finish in National League MVP voting. Our young first baseman, Andres Galaragga, showed flashes of the tremendous player that he would later become. Pascual Perez, a starting pitcher who had demonstrated great potential earlier in his career with the Braves, came to Montreal for the final months of the season and won seven straight decisions.

The surprising success of 1987 turned out to be a mirage, however. Over the next couple of seasons, we slid back to mediocrity, and while the teams around us added missing pieces to drive their playoff hopes, we stayed largely the same. Meanwhile, my style of play started to create wear and tear on my body. I was scuffling through a subpar 1988 season when I hurt my left shoulder diving for a ball in July. I returned to the lineup a few games later but then re-injured the shoulder sliding into second base. I sat out the final month of a season that saw the Mets again win 100 games and the division title.

The late 1980s represented the most frustrating chapter in my career. The hopes of winning a championship in Montreal seemed to fade with each passing day, and I couldn't help but speculate about possible opportunities elsewhere. The question arose whether the victims of collusion would get a do-over at free agency in 1988. "I'll be interested in getting the opportunities I didn't get last year,"

I told reporters at the beginning of the season. "You have to go with what is presented to you. If I say I want to stay in Montreal, the Expos aren't going to offer anything. I just want to leave it wide open and get the chance I didn't have last year. Hopefully, it will be different this time."

As much as I wanted to hear what other teams had to offer, I didn't want to risk winding up in the same position I found myself in after the '86 season. Missing the signing deadline, hearing crickets from other teams, and sitting out the first month of the season took an emotional toll on me. So instead of waiting on an arbitrator's ruling making me eligible to hit the open market, I instead signed a contract extension with the Expos. Montreal had become my second home, and more importantly, ownership didn't force a take-it-or-leave-it offer on me, instead offering a contract that paid market value. I was to receive $2.1 million per season through 1991, and the contract included a team option for a fourth season.

The irony of the situation didn't escape me. After one of the best seasons of my career in 1986, no one offered me anywhere close to that kind of money because of collusion. Now, coming off the most injury-plagued season of my career, I was going to make top dollar. That gave me hope that the Expos were willing to make a financial investment in the rest of the team.

CHAPTER SIX

6

I HAD COME TO BELIEVE that the only way the Expos could compete with the best teams in the National League East would be if everything fell perfectly into place and a lot of guys turned in career years. That's why it came as a pleasant surprise when Expos owner Charles Bronfman publicly conveyed his intention to make whatever moves necessary to turn the team into an immediate contender in 1989. New general manager Dave Dombrowski set out to fulfill Bronfman's wish. With the team at .500 in late May, Dombrowski orchestrated a trade with the Seattle Mariners that brought starting pitcher Mark Langston to Montreal, a bold move considering Langston was more or less a rental due to his upcoming free-agent status. But Dombrowski had listened to Bronfman's marching orders and deemed the deal an important step toward the team's short-term success.

Since Steve Rogers' departure in 1985, the team had struggled to find an ace. Dennis Martinez, who won 15 games for us in 1988, was enjoying a late-career revival in Montreal, but we definitely needed a pitcher to help anchor the rotation. In the left-handed-throwing Langston, we got a guy who had emerged as one of the most talented young pitchers in the game. At the time, it didn't seem like we gave up that much in the deal—three rookie pitchers to be exact. Two of the pitchers, Gene Harris and Brian Holman, didn't go on to have much success in the majors. But the third hurler sent to Seattle, a 6-foot 10-inch lefty named Randy Johnson, blossomed into a 300-game winner and one of the all-time greats. Time and again during his long career, Dombrowski has demonstrated that he's a skilled general manager, but even the best talent evaluators don't have crystal balls. Before he got traded to the Mariners, Randy was 0–4 with a 6.67 ERA. He threw heat, but I'm not sure he knew where the ball was going when it left his hand. For his first few years in Seattle, he continued to struggle to find the strike zone. Then it all started to click for him.

In the months after the trade, the Expos enjoyed some immediate gratification from the deal. Langston won nine of his first 12 decisions, helping to vault us into first place in early August. The Cardinals and Mets, as usual, remained within striking distance, and the Cubs also seemed poised to stay in contention.

As badly as I wanted to achieve personal and team success in Montreal, it was important to reflect on how fortunate I was to play the game I loved, because amid the day-in, day-out grind of a season, you're sometimes reminded of just how fragile a career on the baseball field can be.

The most gruesome moment I witnessed happened during an at-bat against Dave Dravecky of the San Francisco Giants in August 1989. Throughout his career with the Giants and San Diego Padres, the left-handed-throwing Dravecky had always handled me well. In 43 at-bats against him, I only managed nine hits. After the 1988 season, Dravecky underwent surgery to cut out a cancerous tumor in his pitching arm, a procedure that also resulted in the removal of a good bit of muscle from his arm. Somehow he found his way back to a major league pitching mound the following year.

His second start of the season came against us in Montreal. For the first five innings, Dravecky was in complete control, keeping us off the scoreboard and limiting us to just three singles. Things changed abruptly in the sixth inning. Our light-hitting shortstop Damaso Garcia led off the frame with a solo home run. Then Dravecky uncorked a pitch that hit Andres Galarraga. I came to the plate expecting to take a pitch or two to see if Dravecky still had his command. I only saw one pitch, or more accurately, I *heard* it.

The moment Dravecky's first offering left his hand, I and everyone else in Olympic Stadium heard a pop that sounded like a gunshot or firecracker going off. Unfortunately, it was the result of Dravecky's arm bone snapping in half. As the pitch sailed high in the air and to the backstop, Dravecky fell to the ground in agony. In that moment, I had conflicting instincts. Should I go out to the mound to check on the pitcher, or should I tell Andres, who had already advanced to second base, to keep running? You just don't expect to see a man's arm break like that right before your eyes. I had never seen anything like it before and didn't quite know what to do. I hoped it was an injury that Dravecky could come back from, but that pitch turned out to be the last of his career. For what it's worth, he got the win against us that day, but anyone present for it will never forget that moment. Two years after that fateful pitch, Dravecky had his left arm and shoulder amputated in order to prevent the cancer from spreading throughout his body.

A total collapse in August and September doomed us. In the end, the Langston trade made no difference whatsoever to the team. We played .500 ball before we got him, and we played .500 ball after he arrived. He won 12 games for us, and Martinez contributed a team-high 16 victories, but as our final record indicated, everything we did that season was average. We just stopped scoring runs in the final months of the season. And I carried some of the blame for our struggles. Though I stayed healthy in '89, I didn't perform at the same level as I had in previous seasons.

The trade for Langston ended up being a lose-lose-lose for the organization. Not only did we part ways with Randy and drop as many games as we did the year before, we then lost Langston to free agency. That didn't come as much of a surprise. Mark was a California kid who never quite adjusted to life north of the border. It was pretty clear that he and his family wanted to be somewhere closer to home. In December 1989, he signed as a free agent with the California Angels.

A year later, Bronfman abandoned his win-now mentality and sold the team. Dave Van Horne, the Expos' play-by-play man on television for more than 30 years, points to Bronfman's sale of the team as the beginning of the end for baseball in Montreal. "He had built a tight-knit family with the Expos and had a great relationship with the players, but he found out that in the end, it wasn't about family," Van Horne said. "It was about money. That made him very disillusioned."

I understand where Bronfman was coming from. I found the financial side of the game distasteful, too. Sure, I wanted to be paid a fair salary, but I was never strictly motivated by money. Not even close. We saw a lot of finger-pointing in the 1980s, with owners and players accusing each other of letting greed take over the game. Bronfman couldn't find a buyer dedicated to ensuring the long-term health of the franchise, and that was a major blow to the future of baseball in Montreal.

Almost before the ink had dried on the contract I signed after the 1988 season, the Expos seemed willing to move me to another team. I tried to block out the chatter and focus on my job, but I couldn't help but wonder whether the organization had a plan in place to make us a winner. After we lost to the Dodgers in the 1981 NLCS, I thought for sure we'd get another chance to make it to the World Series. But the years passed and we never again came close. Ten years into my career, I faced the reality that the Expos might never get over the top. Every year seemed like a rebuilding year.

An incident that took place during a game in 1990 symbolized how I felt about my future with the club. I was on second base when a teammate hit a double that should have scored me easily. But as I neared home, I tripped and fell flat on my face, forcing me to crawl the last few feet to the plate.

I started looking at the sports pages more closely to see which teams possessed what the Expos used to have but now lacked: a strong core and a vision for the future. The Chicago White Sox, who were coming off a second-place finish in the American League West, caught my eye. They seemed to be moving in the right direction and had a lot of promising young players on their roster. I let Dombrowski know that if he intended to trade me, Chicago would be a preferred destination.

From 1979 to 1990, my years in Montreal, the Expos finished with a .500 or better record 10 out of 12 seasons, an impressive accomplishment for a team that played in Canada and operated on a tight budget. But by 1990, a seven-time All-Star like me was considered a luxury item, especially now that I had entered my thirties. In the final game of the '90 season, I stole three bases in a win against the Cardinals. For a day, it was just like old times.

Then, on December 23, 1990, the Expos traded me, along with two minor-leaguers, to the White Sox for outfielder Ivan Calderon and relief pitcher Barry Jones.

On paper, the trade looked good for both teams. The Expos were looking for a run producer with speed, and the 28-year-old Calderon fit the bill. The White Sox needed a leadoff hitter, a role I looked forward to filling after hitting in the three-hole for most of my final seasons in Montreal. Though I had welcomed the challenge, I never quite adjusted to hitting in the middle of the lineup in Montreal. It changed who I was as a player. Rather than getting on base and running wild, I was expected to knock in runs. Under the circumstances, you might have expected my stolen bases to go way down and my RBIs to go way up, but only the former ended up happening. My batting average also dropped dramatically in the final years of the 1980s.

I had incredibly mixed emotions about leaving Montreal. On the one hand, I knew that it was time to tackle a new challenge in a new place for the second half of my career. My body had started to feel the consequences of playing on the hard Olympic Stadium turf. The grass at the new Comiskey Park in Chicago, which opened during my first year with the White Sox, would give my legs a chance to stay fresh. I also saw that I no longer fit into the Expos' long-term plans, if they had any at all. The addition of Calderon gave the team a very solid outfield that also included Canadian Larry Walker and Marquis Grissom. Dombrowski evidently knew what he was doing. After a disappointing 1991 season, the team reestablished itself as a contender for a brief time. If a strike hadn't ruined the 1994 season, it's very possible that my old team would have faced my new team in the World Series.

Practical considerations aside, I found it difficult to leave the city where I had come of age and become a man. I thought about all the good times I had in Montreal. I also remembered the bad times and the effect they had on shaping my life in a positive way. In my heart, I will always be an Expo. Every time I see that distinctive red-white-and-blue Expos logo, I feel stirrings from the past. As of 2017, I am still the franchise record-holder for runs, triples, walks, and stolen bases. I rank second in games played to Tim Wallach. At some point, those records will probably get claimed by members of the Washington Nationals, the organization the Expos became in 2005 when Major League Baseball determined Montreal could no longer support a team.

My nostalgic feelings for Montreal are that much stronger because the team is no longer there. I'll never forget the 1982 All-Star Game at Olympic Stadium, an evening dominated by Expos. Or my first game back after missing the first month of the 1987 season. The biggest disappointment of my career is that we never got over the hump in Montreal. The 1981 season represented our best chance to bring a championship to Canada, but we fell a game short of reaching the World Series. That is a regret that will always be with me.

My friendships with my former Expos teammates have stood the test of time. In some cases, I've struck up close relationships with guys I only got to know after our respective careers ended. When we played together, I had a ton of respect for Steve Rogers, but he and I didn't talk a lot. Part of that had to do with the fact that position players and pitchers didn't tend to hang out much. In recent years, however, Steve and I have grown close. He's worked for many years for the Major League Baseball Players Association, and whenever I'm in New York City for an event, I get together with Steve and we reminisce about the good ol' Expos days.

As Steve and others have pointed out, history would view the Expos in a much different light if the wild-card format had been in existence in the late 1970s and early 1980s. In that hypothetical universe, we would have made the playoffs four times, instead of just once. Depending on how we performed in the postseason, we might even have been considered a dynasty. Nothing can change history, but that doesn't mean we can't think about what might have been.

Andre Dawson and I also remain extremely close, talking on the phone several times a month and catching up in person whenever our schedules permit. I love Andre like a brother, and I know he feels the same way about me. Warren Cromartie's loyalty to Andre and me knows no bounds. During the years that Hawk and I waited to get elected to the Hall of Fame, Cro served as one of our strongest advocates. At Hawk's induction ceremony, Cro leaned over and told me, "You're gonna be up there in five years, and I'll be sitting with Hawk watching you give your speech." I'm happy to say that he'd be proven right. Unlike players who suited up for other clubs that still exist, my former teammates and I don't gather for annual alumni weekends during the season. But we find ways to keep in touch, to honor our time with the Expos, to give our fans a dose of nostalgia, and to keep the flame of baseball in Montreal burning.

The spring that I joined the White Sox, I made an unusual request of my new team: whenever I got announced over the public address system at games, I wanted to be called "Rock Raines," not "Tim Raines." Looking back, I'm not really sure why I insisted on tinkering with my name. I liked my nickname a lot, so that's probably as good a reason as any. But beyond that, I think it just seemed like a good time to shake things up. New teammates. New league. New name.

My first months as a member of the White Sox were among the most difficult of my career. It took me into May to get my batting average over .200. In the National League, I had seen a lot more fastballs, not because I couldn't hit them, but because pitchers worried about throwing less precise pitches that could lead to a walk and a stolen base. In the American League, where running was a far less significant aspect of the game, pitchers didn't seem too concerned with throwing me a steady diet of breaking balls, and it took me a while to adjust to their habits and tendencies. You can only learn so much from a scouting report. The only way to really learn pitchers is to face them.

I've never been a superstitious person, but I couldn't help but wonder whether I had jinxed myself with the new moniker. It took less than a month for me to reclaim my old name. "Rock Raines was put on waivers," manager Jeff Torborg told reporters before a game in late April, "and Tim Raines was called up." The brief history of "Rock Raines" was immortalized that year on baseball cards issued the following season. I think I still have a few in my collection somewhere.

Things improved for me in late May. I had two four-hit games against Oakland and raised my batting average from the low .200s to nearly .300. Not surprisingly, my stolen-base numbers started going up at the same time. I had hoped to burst out of the gates for my new team, but all things considered, I was pleased that the adjustment process didn't drag on for too long.

As a team, we hung around the .500 mark for the first few months of the season. A hot streak in early August pulled us within a couple of games of first place. But a nine-game losing snap later that month dropped us out of contention. For the season, I hit just .268, but I cracked the 50-stolen-base mark for the first time since 1987. In case you're wondering, in my first season playing in the same league and division as Rickey Henderson, my 51 steals ranked third behind Rickey (58) and Roberto Alomar Jr. (53). In the second-to-last game of the season, Rickey stole four bases to ensure he would end up on top. I think he, too, had heard the constant comparisons between us and made it a priority to lead the league. I stole just one base in our last 10 games, sticking to my mantra of only trying to swipe a bag if it helped my team to win.

I don't know if it was irony or not, but while I tried to steal bases for the White Sox, a group of criminals was breaking into my unoccupied off-season home in Florida and stealing jewelry, stereo equipment, and anything else they could find inside. After the third such burglary, Virginia and I decided to sell the house. One of the downsides of spending much of the year away from home is that the bad guys know when you're gone.

The White Sox finished in second place with a record of 87–75, eight games behind the division-winning Twins. But I looked around the clubhouse and liked what I saw. First baseman Frank Thomas and third baseman Robin Ventura had the look of future stars. In his first full season in the majors, Frank hit .318 with 32 home runs and 109 RBIs. Robin also knocked in 100 runs. Lance Johnson and I formed a nice combo at the top of the lineup. And from a leadership standpoint, it helped to have 43-year-old future Hall of Famer Carlton Fisk in the clubhouse. At an age when most catchers are 10 years into retirement, Carlton was still strapping on his gear a hundred times a year. It inspired me that a player I used to look up to was still an active major-leaguer as I entered my second decade of play. As a Cincinnati Reds fan growing up, I clearly remembered Carlton, then of the Red Sox, hitting that famous home run against the Reds in Game 6 of the 1975 World Series. I have special respect for guys who maintain a high level of performance long after the peak years of their career have ended. The only way to pull that off is to possess an extraordinary amount of heart and dedication. On days when knuckleballer Charlie Hough pitched for the White Sox, the combined age of our battery was 86! Despite his advanced years, Charlie ended up throwing the second-most innings for us in '91.

In July of that year, Carlton became the oldest player ever to get a hit in an All-Star Game. He, shortstop Ozzie Guillen, and pitcher Jack McDowell represented the White Sox for the American League that year. I really admired Ozzie as a player. He had an incredible passion for the game and hustled his butt off. From a pitching standpoint, McDowell was starting to come into his own. In his third full season in the majors, he went 17–10 and led the league in complete games. It was pretty clear that we needed another solid starting pitcher or two if we hoped to compete for a title. Fortunately, we had a couple of 21-year-old kids, Alex Fernandez and Wilson Alvarez, who seemed poised to take major steps forward.

One of the best things about the '91 season was playing alongside Bo Jackson, who signed with the White Sox less than a week before opening day and three months after he suffered a hip injury with the Los Angeles Raiders that ended his football career. I absolutely loved Bo as a football player and remember my disappointment when he decided not to sign with my favorite NFL team, the Tampa Bay Buccaneers, who drafted him first overall out of Auburn University in 1986. I honestly had no idea that Bo even played baseball until he announced he was signing with the Kansas City Royals instead of the Bucs. Amazingly, he got called up to the majors the same year the Royals drafted him. He had so much raw talent. The way he crushed home runs and chased down fly balls in the outfield amazed me. I couldn't get past the fact that this guy was a football player moonlighting as a baseball player—or maybe it was the other way around. He made the American League All-Star team in 1989, and the next year he made the Pro Bowl as a member of the Raiders.

Any baseball player who ever dreamt of someday playing in the NFL put Bo on a pedestal, because he became one of the few athletes to actually star in both sports at the professional level. To me, the fact that he played running back made his accomplishment that much more impressive. Unlike former major-leaguers Deion

Sanders and Brian Jordan, who played defensive positions on the football field, Bo took hits, rather than dishing them out. If he hadn't gotten hurt playing football in '91, I think he had a chance to become a Hall of Famer in both sports.

Despite the huge amount of notoriety he gained from his Nike ad campaigns, Bo came across as one of the most humble people I ever met. Based on his accomplishments, he should have had a supersized ego. Instead, he couldn't have been more down to earth. Most people wouldn't have been able to continue playing baseball after experiencing the type of injury Bo did, but his resolve to get back to the majors drove him to do whatever it took to rehabilitate his hip. His brute strength helped with the process. But his pride was what made it possible in the end for him to come back. An athlete like Bo comes along once in a lifetime. Bo got on the field for us at the end of the '91 season. I had a lot of fun in his presence and looked forward to seeing him on the field more often in the years to come.

Another added bonus of going to the White Sox is that I got a chance to live in the same city as my friend Andre Dawson, who had played for the Chicago Cubs for the past four seasons. I knew our respective schedules wouldn't allow for much socializing during the season, but I still decided to get an apartment closer to the North Side of town where he lived, even if it meant a longer commute to Comiskey Park. We didn't see each other much, but it was nice to hear Andre's name when I watched the local TV news. This was before interleague play, so the only time we got to face off against each other during our years in Chicago was in the annual "Windy City Classic" exhibition game.

Back in Montreal, the Expos struggled through a 90-loss season and fired Buck Rodgers in June. Calderon, my replacement in left field, had a solid year, hitting .300 and making an All-Star team for the only time in his career. Based on my so-so season and Calderon's breakout year, people were quick to say that the Expos got the better of the deal. But it's difficult to assess a trade after just one season. Calderon rarely saw the field due to injuries in 1992 and was traded away after his second season in Montreal. He retired from the game a year later. Tragically, he was shot to death in his native Puerto Rico in 2003.

After the '91 season, Torborg resigned as White Sox manager in order to take the same job with the Mets. We liked Jeff and he liked us, but going to New York gave him a chance to be closer to his family. Both he and his wife were from New Jersey. Gene Lamont, who had never managed in the majors but had ample experience as a coach, got the nod as his replacement.

The biggest on-field development of the '92 season involved a swap of outfielders right before the start of the season. We sent 23-year-old Sammy Sosa across town to the Cubs and got former American League MVP George Bell in return. In my limited time playing with Sammy, I observed a guy with a lot of talent who appeared unwilling to put in the hard work necessary to become a star. Maybe he needed a few more seasons under his belt to mature. I just know that he clashed with our hitting instructor, Walt Hriniak, one of the most respected coaches in the game. Trading Sammy made sense at the time, just as the Expos trading Randy Johnson for Mark Langston in 1989 made sense from a win-now standpoint. You never know how trades will work out in the long run. George didn't have the impact White Sox general manager Ron Schueler hoped he would, but it was still a trade worth making.

We didn't stay healthy enough to make 1992 a banner year. Guillen's desire to catch every ball hit in his general vicinity got him into trouble early in the season. In an April game, Mel Hall of the Yankees hit a blooper to short left field that Ozzie and I both pursued at full speed. As I slid for the ball, Ozzie slammed into me, causing him to flip over. The ball fell in between us for a double. Worse, Ozzie tore ligaments in his knee and missed the rest of the season.

Lamont produced the same results as Torborg had the year before. Instead of winning 87 games, we won 86, which put us in third place in the American League West. I boosted my batting average by 26 points, a sign that I had fully adjusted to AL pitching. The next challenge for me and the team was proving we had what it took to win the division.

CHAPTER SEVEN

7

NO MATTER HOW WELL THE Expos played while I was in Montreal, the city always remained a hockey town first and foremost. In 1981, Guy Lafleur and the rest of the Montreal Canadiens were a few games into their season by the time we took the field to open the National League Championship Series. They were blasting the competition off the ice, winning games by scores of 9–0 and 10–4. In October, there were more people talking about the Stanley Cup than baseball's postseason.

Don't get me wrong. We got huge and enthusiastic crowds for our playoff games against the Dodgers that fall, but I think the sting of our loss in that series didn't hit the local fans as hard as it would have in a town where baseball was king, or at least a close second to football. The Canadiens, by the way, had the third-best record in the NHL during the 1981–82 season, but they got eliminated in the first round of the playoffs by the Quebec Nordiques. It was a tough year all around for sports fans in Montreal.

From the moment I arrived in Chicago, I could tell how much the city loved its baseball, both on the North and South Sides, despite neither the Cubs nor the White Sox giving fans much to cheer about over the years. The respective World Series droughts of the two Windy City teams became legendary. I was standing in the first-base coaching box when the White Sox finally broke through with a title in 2005. And the Cubs...well, I think most baseball fans, with the exception of those in Cleveland, enjoyed the outcome of the 2016 World Series. Finally, long-suffering Cubs fans could celebrate a championship.

During my seasons in Chicago, the White Sox remained near the top of the league in attendance, and the media spotlight was far more intense than it had been in Montreal. Little went on in or around the clubhouse that an enterprising reporter didn't pick up on. When a team performs poorly, it opens itself up to scrutiny and second-guessing. A winning team, however, can bask in the glow of lots of positive attention. The latter happened to the White Sox in 1993.

Before I could experience the thrill of my first non-strike-year pennant run, I had to learn a valuable lesson about taking care of my body. Earlier in my career, I perfected the ability to slide headfirst into bases. I found that diving into a base with my arms outstretched gave me the best chance of beating a throw. An incident that took place in our fourth game of the '93 season prompted me to reevaluate the virtues of sliding this way.

After leading off a game against the New York Yankees with a walk, I took off for second base and went in headfirst to beat the throw from catcher Mike Stanley. In the process, I jammed my thumb into the bag. As soon as it happened, I knew I had hurt myself, but I tried to remain in the game. I didn't understand the magnitude of the injury until I went to the outfield the next half inning and found I couldn't grip the baseball. I missed the next six weeks of the season with a torn ligament. The incident served as a wake-up call. I wasn't going to completely swear off sliding headfirst, but I did determine that extending the longevity of my career depended on not subjecting my body to excessive risk.

I went to the White Sox after the 1990 season in order to help them win a championship. In my third season with the club, we were ready to make the leap. The White Sox drafted extremely well from 1987 to 1990, selecting Jack McDowell, Robin Ventura, Frank Thomas, and Alex Fernandez with their first-round picks. That's a lot of homegrown talent to build around, a strategy that usually pays dividends—just ask the Expos of the early 1980s. But to get to the next level, the White Sox believed they needed to bring in some players from the outside, something the Expos were generally reluctant to do. That's where I entered the picture. Early on in a season, you pick up on whether the team you're playing for has the aura of a winner. The '93 team definitely had that feel. That's what made missing six weeks in April and May so frustrating. I felt I had let the team down.

In my first five games back from the disabled list, I reached base with a hit or walk 12 times. But in a scenario that would have been unimaginable just a few years earlier, I didn't steal a single base in that period. In 1993, my game changed. I stole a career-low 21 bases as I adopted a more cautious approach on the base paths following my injury. I realized I couldn't help my team if I wasn't on the field, and the best way to ensure I stayed in uniform was to protect my body.

Frank Thomas' dislike for the running game also influenced that adaptation. Frank never wanted me to try and steal if he was at the plate, even in obvious running situations. I liked to joke that he'd get mad if I took off for second base on a 3-2 count with two outs. He felt that if I successfully swiped second, the opposing team would be tempted to give him a free pass with first base open. Like any slugger, he wanted to take his cuts, but not at the expense of going after bad pitches. Frank led the American League in walks in four of the five seasons that I played with him. A good number of those walks were intentional, but I like to think we struck a happy balance between maintaining a running game and letting the Big Hurt swing his mighty bat.

To this day, Frank still wonders why I even contemplated running when he was up to bat. "I could hit anything," he tells me. "Why run when I was probably going to hit a two-run homer or a ball in the gap? You'd come around to score either way, so why not do it the easy way?"

Big Frank wasn't known for his defense, but he more than made up for that with his bat. Still, I liked to have a little fun at his expense whenever he booted a grounder or made an errant throw. We had a lot of serious-minded veterans in our clubhouse, and I think Frank appreciated my willingness to lighten the mood. It sent the signal that it was okay for him to laugh, too.

Over the grind of a long season, it's difficult to recognize in real time what events will transcend the moment and stand the test of time. The postseason is different. Those images stay with us through the years. Yogi Berra jumping into Don Larsen's arms after Larsen pitched a perfect game in the 1956 World Series is a prime example, as are so many other performances that turned players into October heroes. As a former Expo, I can attest to the fact that Rick Monday's home run in the deciding game of the 1981 National

League Championship Series is burned in the memory of everyone who played in that game.

From April through September, you get into the routine of showing up at the ballpark and trying to put one in the win column. You never expect a normal Wednesday night in August to produce a highlight (or lowlight) for the ages. But that's exactly what happened during a White Sox–Rangers game in Texas in 1993.

Just mention the names Robin Ventura and Nolan Ryan, and most baseball fans immediately know what you're referring to. Not only that, they can immediately visualize the incident in question. I saw it from the visitors' dugout and can very clearly still picture the 26-year-old Ventura charging the mound to confront the 46-year-old Ryan, in his 27th season in the majors, who had just drilled him in the right arm with a pitch.

We'll never know why Nolan hit Robin. Maybe what he said after the game and in the years that followed—that the pitch simply got away from him—is true. Or maybe Robin or one of our teammates did something to irritate him. All that mattered in that moment was that Robin believed that Nolan did it intentionally.

Nobody would have ever given a second thought to the play if Robin hadn't decided to communicate his displeasure to Nolan. As Robin took a couple of steps toward first base, you could almost see the wheels in his head turning. He could either continue up the baseline or confront Ryan. I've never asked Robin to explain why he did what he did, but I had an excellent view of the incident, so here's my take on what happened: after Robin took a few steps toward Ryan, he had a change of heart. And once he actually got to the mound, he realized that wasn't where he wanted to be. Robin was a mild-mannered guy and not someone you would have expected to challenge an opposing player to a fight. But in the heat of that moment, he decided that charging the mound made sense.

Ryan apparently still had memories years earlier of being roughed up by Dave Winfield in a bench-clearing brawl, an experience that led to a vow to be ready the next time a hitter came at him. Nolan's tenacity combined with Robin's tentativeness spelled bad news for Robin, who lunged at his adversary and promptly got put into a headlock that enabled Nolan to land several blows to the head. Both teams spilled onto the field and order was quickly restored, but the decisiveness of Ryan's victory in the fight made it a part of baseball history.

My teammates and I had a few laughs at Robin's expense, and he took our jokes in stride. It was probably harder for him to deal with the many wisecracks I'm sure he still hears in airports and on the street. The rise of the Internet guaranteed that he would never live down the incident.

Since we're on the subject, I should probably mention that never in my 23 years in the majors did I charge the mound. The main reason for that is that I'm not a confrontational guy by nature. The other reason is that I didn't get hit that many times in my career—just 42 times to be exact. As a switch-hitter, not a lot of pitches came in on me. That limited the number of times I got hit unintentionally. The only occasion where I believe a pitcher purposely hit me came in the 1980s when Rick Reuschel of the Pittsburgh Pirates plunked me with a fastball. It didn't hurt that much—Reuschel didn't throw that hard—so it never occurred to me to go out to the mound. I don't remember why Reuschel threw at me, but I do remember singling, doubling, and tripling off him a couple of years later en route to hitting for the cycle. That was the best revenge.

The Ryan-Ventura incident obviously stands out in my mind as the most memorable brawl I took part in. The other one I recall happened when my Expos teammate Spike Owen got hit by Houston Astros reliever Larry Andersen in the Astrodome. Andersen was a lot bigger than Spike and easily fended off his attack. Spike ended up on the bottom of a huge pile of players. As I approached the scene, I noticed that an Astros player had a handful of Spike's hair and was tugging on it. This tactic crossed the line, so I grabbed the guy and pulled him out of the pile and took a swing at him. That was the only time I ever threw a punch in a baseball fight, but I felt it was an appropriate reaction. Most of the time, I found someone I knew on the other team and went off to the side of the gathering to have a friendly conversation until everything settled down.

The Rangers got the better of us in that August brawl, but we got the last laugh by beating them out for the American League West crown in 1993. In late September, we clinched the division at home against the Seattle Mariners. The celebration that night at Comiskey is something I'll always remember. Lots of hugs, lots of champagne, and not a lot of sleep.

What separated the '93 club that won 94 games from the '92 team that won 86 games? For one thing, we found an everyday right fielder in Ellis Burks to contribute to the offense. In my first two seasons with the team, we used a platoon system in right that included Sammy Sosa, Dan Pasqua, Mike Huff, and Warren Newson, none of whom established himself as an everyday player. In Ellis, who signed with the White Sox after six seasons in Boston,

Gene Lamont got a right fielder he could plug into the lineup every day. Ellis didn't need to carry the offense. Frank, who was the American League MVP in '93, and Robin were doing that already. Ellis just needed to put up solid numbers, which he did, finishing the season with 17 home runs and 74 RBIs. I did my fair share, as well, hitting over .300 for the first time since 1987.

On the mound, 1993 saw the hoped-for emergence of Fernandez and Wilson Alvarez, who won a combined 33 games. Rookie Jason Bere chipped in another 12 victories. McDowell took care of the rest, winning 22 games and the American League Cy Young award. General manager Ron Schueler got a lot of criticism for not signing a big-name free-agent pitcher before the season, but it turned out we didn't need one. Our pitching staff had a great year, and when we held a lead late in the game, we tended to finish off the win. In his first season as our full-time closer, Roberto Hernandez saved 38 games.

We had worked together the entire season to get this far. Now we hoped to get the White Sox back to the World Series for the first time since 1959. To make that happen, we needed to play to our full potential to beat the defending champion Toronto Blue Jays in the American League Championship Series. That Toronto team had power and speed and could score runs in bunches. Designated hitter Paul Molitor was an MVP candidate, and Joe Carter, Roberto Alomar, and John Olerud all had great seasons. It spoke volumes about the strength of their offense that Rickey Henderson had become one of the easier outs in the lineup. The Blue Jays hitters definitely had us beat from an experience standpoint. Unlike our guys, most of the players on Toronto's roster had played in the postseason before. But despite our lack of big-game experience, we felt we matched up well against a team whose pitching ace was untested 24-year-old Pat Hentgen.

We opened the ALCS with two games at Comiskey Park, hoping to get out to an early lead in the best-of-seven series with McDowell on the mound. Instead we dug ourselves a hole, losing 7–3. Thanks to the wildness of Toronto's starting pitcher, Juan Guzman, we had plenty of chances to put up crooked numbers on the scoreboard, but we couldn't take advantage of Guzman's eight walks (three of them to Frank), one hit batsman, and three wild pitches. In my first postseason game in over a decade, I went 2-for-5 with an RBI and a stolen base.

Then in the middle of Game 2, a huge piece of sports news broke in Chicago. But it didn't have anything to do with us...at least for the time being. We got overshadowed by rumors that Michael Jordan was retiring from the NBA at the age of 30. No figure in American sports had a larger profile than Michael, and Chicagoans absolutely worshipped him for leading the Bulls to three consecutive NBA championships. His decision to step away from the game three weeks before the start of the new season left the entire city, and probably most of the world, in shock. I included myself among his fans. During my first year in town, with the Bulls on the verge of their first championship, I got a chance to meet Michael and his teammates at the old Chicago Stadium. I immediately liked his laid-back presence and easy smile.

The timing of Michael's announcement didn't bother me. He had earned the right to break the news whenever he wanted. But Jerry Reinsdorf, who owned both the White Sox and the Bulls, felt otherwise and asked Schueler to apologize to us on his behalf for Michael upstaging that day's game against the Blue Jays. The sportswriters covering our series couldn't resist getting our thoughts on the news. Ozzie Guillen, never one to hold back his thoughts as a player or later a manager, told reporters, "If I had his money, I wouldn't be here, believe me. I don't blame him at all. There's too much pressure every day in every city, and he can't enjoy it. I bet he never enjoyed basketball during the playoffs."

The writers could always count on Ozzie for a good quote. I can't speak for him, but I enjoyed the pressure of playoff baseball and wanted my team to remain in the postseason for as long as possible. Unfortunately, we took another step backward in Game 2, losing 3–1. Fernandez pitched well for us, but we couldn't capitalize on numerous scoring opportunities against Blue Jays pitcher Dave Stewart. You can't win games if you don't get timely hits. In the first two games of the series, we left a total of 23 runners on base.

It's funny how losing two games in October can change the entire mood of a team and a fan base. Tired of seeing so many runners stranded on the base paths, our frustrated fans serenaded us with boos in Game 2. And shortly before we boarded a plane for Toronto, clubhouse dissension started to emerge. Bo Jackson, who didn't appear in either game in Chicago, blasted Lamont for keeping him out of the lineup. "The last two days, we've been one man short, and it shows," Bo told reporters after our second loss to Toronto. Bo felt Gene should have inserted him in the Game 2 lineup or at least called on him to pinch-hit with men on base later in the game. The fans were chanting his name, after all. Part of the reason Bo got benched was that Frank had an injured elbow that limited him to Bo's usual assignment, the designated hitter role. Gene didn't take kindly to Bo's comments, telling reporters, "We win together, we lose together. If Bo plays in a game and strikes out four times, I hope no other player would say we played one player short."

Despite neutralizing Alomar and Henderson, who went a combined 0-for-17 in Games 1 and 2, we still found ourselves in a giant hole, needing to win two of three games in Toronto to get the series back to Chicago. The good news, if any could be found, was that we had the best road record in baseball during the season. In my heart, I believed we could come back and win.

That probably wasn't going to happen if we went down 3–0 in the series, however. We needed to win, and the city needed us to win. Michael Jordan had left the building, Mike Ditka wasn't coaching the Bears for the first time in 12 years, and the last thing a sad sports city needed was a quick exit by the White Sox in the ALCS. Frank summed it up well when he said before Game 3, "We've played just terribly. That hasn't been us out there." Even the Blue Jays noticed that we weren't playing or acting like a team that ran away with the division title. One of their players said that we looked uptight.

Gene made one significant adjustment for Game 3. With Frank back at first base, he put Bo in the starting lineup. It was a good move in my opinion. Not only could Bo give us a much-needed offensive jolt, but it also eased the tension that had hung over the clubhouse since Bo and Gene bad-mouthed each other in the papers.

As it turned out, we didn't need Bo, who went hitless in Game 3. After both teams went down quietly in the first two innings, we broke through for five two-out runs against Hentgen in the top of the third. We did everything in that inning that we failed to do in Chicago, scoring all of our runs with two outs, on five singles and two walks. Alvarez gave up a run in the bottom half of the inning, but the Blue Jays didn't score again. Unlike in the first two games of the series, we executed and the Blue Jays didn't. In the clubhouse after our 6–1 victory, there was an incredible feeling of satisfaction and relief. I went 4-for-5 in Game 3 and felt locked in at the plate. I could hardly wait to get back on the field the following evening.

It's funny what storylines the media latch onto. The Rickey Henderson comparisons I had heard my entire career followed me into the playoffs. A year earlier, Rickey had been a member of an Oakland A's team that fell in six games to the Blue Jays in the ALCS. To help bolster their playoff chances in '93, Toronto made a deal for Rickey at the trading deadline. He hit just .215 down the stretch, but he still managed to work a lot of walks and steal a lot of bases. The "Rock vs. Man of Steal" subplot appealed to reporters, one of whom asked me, "Do you think you've outplayed Rickey Henderson in this series?" For those keeping score at home, I did outplay Rickey, who didn't do a whole lot against us, but that was the furthest thing from my mind during the series.

Let me rephrase that. How I performed compared to Rickey was the *second*-furthest thing from my mind. At least that subplot related to what I was doing on the field. The same couldn't be said about my impending free agency. But my contract status with the White Sox apparently weighed on the minds of reporters, because they kept asking me whether I planned on re-signing with the team after the season. I swatted the question away by explaining that this was something that would be dealt with *after the season*. I guess I couldn't blame the journalists for asking, but they couldn't blame me for staying focused on the task at hand: getting to the World Series.

You never can predict what might transpire in the postseason. Sometimes sluggers and ace pitchers go into series-long slumps and slap-hitters and fifth starters have career weeks. Game 4 of the ALCS turned Lance Johnson into an unlikely hero. Don't get me wrong, Lance had established himself as a valuable part of our team, a guy who could get on and steal a base hitting anywhere in the lineup. But he wasn't known for his power. In fact, he didn't hit a single long ball in 579 regular season plate appearances in '93. Fourteen triples, but zero home runs. So imagine our surprise when Lance put us up in Game 4 with a two-run shot off Todd Stottlemyre in the second inning. The Blue Jays answered with three runs in the third inning to take the lead, but Lance helped spearhead another big inning in the sixth with a two-out, two-run triple. Toronto scored a run in the bottom half of the inning, but I prevented them from tying the game by throwing Alomar out at the plate on a Carter single. We went on to win 7–4, and just like that, the series was tied at two games apiece.

I picked up another three hits in Game 4 and I also came close to getting ejected for challenging an umpire who blew a call. The incident happened in the third inning after I hit a leadoff double. I went into second base standing up but then got pushed off the bag by Blue Jays shortstop Tony Fernandez as he applied the tag. Second-base umpire Ken Kaiser didn't see the push, however, and ruled that I overran the base. Everyone at home could clearly see that he missed the call, but we didn't have instant-replay reviews back then, so all I could do was plead my case to Kaiser. In the course of expressing myself to him, we got up close and personal. In the heat of the moment, I was pretty steamed. My words didn't sway him, but at least he didn't toss me. Fortunately, the blown call didn't have a bearing on the outcome of the game.

After our messy performance in Chicago to start the series, I don't think anybody expected us to go to Toronto and come away with two wins in a row. It looked like we were in one of those ruts that often result in quick playoff exits. But we had confidence in ourselves, and with the pressure on, we played with urgency. We still had work to do, but regardless of the outcome of the next game, we guaranteed ourselves at least another game in Chicago.

Playing in a packed ballpark with more than 50,000 people added to our challenge in Toronto. I don't think any stadium in baseball got as loud as the SkyDome, where the Blue Jays had led the American League in attendance every year since 1989. For me, it wasn't quite a homecoming, but playing north of the border reminded me of something I picked up during my years in Montreal. The crowd noise in Canadian stadiums had a distinct sound. To my trained ears, the cheers of Canadian fans were more high-pitched and piercing than their American counterparts. And it felt like the entire country was embracing the Blue Jays' run at a second straight World Series. A lot of Jays fans had probably cheered for me when I wore an Expos uniform, but now that I was a member of a White Sox team trying to knock Toronto out of the postseason, I'm sure they thought of me as "Tim who?"

I felt good about our chances of going undefeated in Toronto. Game 5 featured a rematch of the series opener, with McDowell going up against Guzman. Jack didn't have his best stuff in Game 1, but there was no one we would have rather had on the mound than him. He was the presumptive Cy Young award recipient and the winningest pitcher of the early '90s for a reason. But in Game 5, Jack found himself in trouble from the get-go, giving up five hits, three walks, and three runs in 2⅓ innings before Lamont gave him the hook. The Blue Jays had Jack's number. His struggles in the '93 ALCS remind me of Clayton Kershaw's four straight losses against the St. Louis Cardinals in the 2013 and 2014 postseasons. One bad inning can cost your team an opportunity to advance, and a loss in a big game can erase the memories of a great regular season.

Guzman, who couldn't find the strike zone four days earlier, suddenly looked like the greatest control pitcher of all time, walking only one batter and giving up just three hits in seven innings of work. Toronto scored a single run in each of the first four innings. We didn't get our first hit off Guzman until Burks hit a solo home run in the fifth. Toronto scored another run in the seventh to extend its lead to four runs. But we went down fighting. Ventura's two-run home run in the top of the ninth brought us within two, and following a walk to Burks, Bo came up as the potential tying run. Maybe sitting out the first two games of the series threw off his rhythm, or maybe he just fell into a slump at the wrong time, but Bo's only trip to the postseason didn't go well. In what turned out to be his last at-bat of the series, he struck out swinging against Blue Jays closer Duane Ward to end Game 5.

Trailing 3–2 in the series, we again had our backs up against the wall. But I saw no reason why we couldn't go back to Chicago and win two games in a row.

Lamont had some tactical decisions to make prior to Game 6. The highest profile of those choices involved who would be the designated hitter. He could have picked Bo, who had the potential to bust out at any time, despite his struggles in Toronto. Then there was George Bell, whose major slump at the end of the season had relegated him to the bench for the first five games of the series. George wanted to play against his former team and communicated that fact to everyone through the media. Gene's third option, Warren Newson, didn't have Bo and George's name recognition or history of accomplishment, but he had established himself as a pretty good pinch hitter and occasional DH for us.

If the fans had been filling out the lineup card, they definitely would have penciled in the former league MVP or the two-sport superstar. But Gene felt that Warren, who batted left-handed, matched up better against Stewart than the right-handed hitting Bo or Bell. The other lineup switch came at catcher, where Gene benched Ron Karkovice, who was hitless in the series, for Mike LaValliere.

The only previous time that I played in the postseason, with the Expos in 1981, the weather in Montreal was anything but summer-like. That's just the reality of postseason baseball. The boys of summer become the boys of fall, especially in northern and midwestern cities, as the heat and humidity of July and August give way to the chill of October. The temperature inside the SkyDome in Toronto had been perfect, of course. Now it was back to the natural elements. The forecast for Game 5 in Chicago called for temperatures in the high 30s and strong winds.

I'm a Florida guy, and in many ways, always will be. I like the warmth. That's why I've lived in the Phoenix area for years. But I didn't mind playing in the extreme heat or cold and I had experience with both. There were games in St. Louis when the temperature on the artificial turf reached 120 degrees and we had to soak our cleats between innings in a mixture of ammonia and water to cool them off. Having played many years in Montreal prior to the completion of Olympic Stadium's roof, I also knew all about suiting up in wintry weather. But once I stepped between the lines and the adrenaline started flowing, I tended not to think too much about the atmospheric conditions.

That night in Chicago tested my limits, however. Despite bundling up in six or seven layers of clothing, including a wool shirt and windbreaker under my jersey, I couldn't help but feel just how blustery it was. I don't think I've ever been colder in my entire life. At the plate, I tried to avoid getting jammed or hitting a ball off the end of the bat. Anyone who has ever played baseball in frigid weather knows that causes you to lose feeling in your hands. After coming in off the field, I immediately went to one of the heat blowers that had been installed on each end of the dugout. As long as I kept moving, I felt fine. But there's a lot of standing around in baseball, so most of the time I just felt cold.

As I said, you never know who will rise to the occasion in the postseason to help get his team over the top. In Toronto's case, that player was 36-year-old Dave Stewart, a perennial Cy Young candidate in the late 1980s whose career appeared to be on the downturn when he signed as a free agent with the Blue Jays before the '93 season. In Stewart and Jack Morris, Toronto had a couple of seasoned veterans at the back of the rotation for most of the season. Neither pitched like they had in their prime, and Morris didn't appear in the postseason due to injury, but Blue Jays manager Cito Gaston called on Stewart to make two starts in the ALCS. The strategy made sense. Stewart had proven he could pitch in big-game situations, most memorably when his four victories for the Oakland A's in the 1989 postseason earned him World Series MVP honors.

The Blue Jays helped Stewart out by scoring two runs in the second inning of Game 6 to take the lead. We tied the game with a pair of runs in the third, but Toronto went ahead again with a run in the fourth. Then both starting pitchers settled in. Fernandez kept us in the game, but we just couldn't break through against Stewart, who pitched into the eighth inning. The score still stood at 3–2 going into the ninth inning. And that's when Toronto blew it open, scoring three runs on a Devon White home run and a Molitor triple. Newson's ninth-inning home run brought us a little closer and provided the only RBI we got from the designated hitter position during the series. I flied out for the final out of the game. And that was that. For his two wins in the series, Stewart took home MVP honors.

I knew I reached base a lot during the series, but I wasn't keeping track of my stats. As it turned out, I hit safely in all six games and went 12-for-27 in the series. I prided myself on being a player who came to compete every single time I went out on the field, regardless of whether a game was "meaningful" or not. Every game had meaning to me, and I like to think I approached them all with equal preparedness.

That being said, postseason baseball has an undeniable level of excitement that you just don't find during the grind of the regular season. And I loved the thrill and pressure of squaring off against

(top) Here I am with my Pony League team when I was just a kid. Baseball was actually my second love when I was growing up; my first was football.

(right) Before I was called up to Montreal, I spent time in the minor leagues with the Denver Bears. That team had a lot of major league talent on it, including future Expos Bill Gullickson and Tim Wallach.

Once I reached the majors, I continued to put my speed to good use. I also got to play against some of my heroes, such as the great Joe Morgan. (AP Images)

There is no way I would be where I am today without the mentoring and friendship of the great Andre Dawson. Hawk and I remain close to this day. (AP Images)

Despite not entering the game until the sixth inning, I took home the MVP award in the 1987 All-Star Game after collecting three hits, including the game winner in the 13th inning. (AP Images)

Montreal traded me to the Chicago White Sox in 1990, where I set the table for future Hall of Famer Frank Thomas. We might have won a World Series together if not for the players strike in 1994. (AP Images)

By 1996, I had moved on to the New York Yankees, where I was fortunate enough to win my first World Series championship. It meant so much to me to finally reach the top of the mountain alongside teammates like Daryl Strawberry and Derek Jeter. (AP Images)

(right) Although I had announced my retirement from baseball, I came back in 2000 and joined the Somerset Patriots for a few games in the hope of being named to the United States Olympic team. I was disappointed when it didn't work out—it would have been an honor to represent my country. (AP Images)

(below) I was back with the Expos in 2001 and got the thrill of a lifetime when my son Tim Jr. and I played against each other in a spring training game. Later that season, I was traded to the Orioles and we played together in a major league game, only the second father-son duo to accomplish that feat in major league history. (AP Images)

My son Andre could run like the wind, just like his dad. Andre played American Legion baseball as a teenager and was a wide receiver in college. (Raines family)

My parents, Ned Sr. and Florence Raines, raised my siblings and me to have love in our hearts. (Randy Grossman)

I was overwhelmed when the Expos retired my jersey No. 30 in 2004. I will always have the fondest memories of Montreal, and in my heart, I will always be an Expo. (AP Images)

Three of the greatest base stealers of all time: Vince Coleman, Rickey Henderson, and yours truly. (Randy Grossman)

Shannon and I were married in 2007, and we welcomed our beautiful twin baby girls, Amelie and Ava, in 2010. (Randy Grossman)

On January 18, 2017, I got the phone call many thought might never come: I had been elected to the National Baseball Hall of Fame. For me, it was the fulfillment of an unimaginable dream. It was even more special to have Shannon, Amelie, and Ava by my side. (Randy Grossman)

one of the best teams in the league with so much on the line. The Blue Jays had a great team, but I think we were every bit as good as them. It was a series we should have won. Instead, Toronto went on to beat the Philadelphia Phillies in the World Series on Joe Carter's walk-off home run in the bottom of the ninth inning of Game 6.

At the age of 34, I was running out of opportunities to play in a World Series. But I looked ahead to 1994 with great hope. Our roster looked to remain largely intact, giving us a legitimate chance of making it back to the postseason. Little did I know that I was in for one of the biggest disappointments of my life, and it wasn't because of anything that happened on the field.

CHAPTER EIGHT

8

MY DECISION TO RE-SIGN WITH Chicago after the 1993 season was an easy one. I had unfinished business to tend to.

After falling just short of the World Series the previous season, the White Sox still had the pieces in place to compete for a championship. In recognition of my solid play the past three seasons, the White Sox rewarded me with a three-year contract extension worth $500,000 more than my first deal with the club. I felt invested in my new team and city. The White Sox may not have garnered the level of national attention that the Cubs received, but they had a very loyal fan base and a strong desire to win a World Series.

We had yet to report to Sarasota for spring training when more Michael Jordan news grabbed the headlines. This time, however, the story pertained directly to us. In his second shocking announcement in four months, Michael told the world that he planned to embark on a baseball career, and to that end, had signed a minor league contract with the White Sox. Unbeknownst to the public, Michael, a former high school baseball player in his native North Carolina, had been working out at Comiskey Park to ready himself for this new challenge. When White Sox owner Jerry Reinsdorf informed the team of Michael's plan, most of us weren't sure whether Michael was serious about becoming a baseball player or if it was just a publicity stunt.

About a week before Michael dropped his news, Bo Jackson signed as a free agent with the California Angels. One two-sport athlete had left us, but another was on the way.

When Michael arrived in big league camp on February 15, it seemed that every member of the sports media showed up to greet him. And for the duration of camp, the flashbulbs never stopped popping. That meant an early wake-up call for photographers because Michael reported to the facility every morning at 7:00 AM to work with White Sox hitting instructor Walt Hriniak, who I considered the best hitting coach in baseball. "If you're one second late, you don't hit," Walt let him know on the first day they worked together. Michael always showed up early.

In an attempt to control the circus-like coverage surrounding our new player, the White Sox decided to limit Michael's press availability to every third day. But manager Gene Lamont wisely overruled that decision, arguing that the rest of the team would be inundated with questions about him on the two days he wasn't talking to reporters himself. Some teams may not have responded well to a newbie hogging all of the attention at camp. But it didn't bother us, because we didn't have big egos on our team and this rookie wasn't just anybody.

Rather than getting upset about the fixation on Michael, I kind of enjoyed the crazy atmosphere that broke out around us. Of all the spring trainings I attended during my career, it was by far the most interesting. Michael's experiment intrigued me. No one doubted his athletic prowess, but I and a lot of other people wondered whether he could make the transition from one professional sport to another. Every baseball player will tell you that hitting a baseball consistently well is the most difficult act in sports. Michael could run, obviously. And I figured he could master tracking down balls in the outfield. But could he hit? That's what I was anxious to see.

I got to know Michael pretty well that spring working with him in the outfield. He loved to crack jokes, but during drills, he locked into the task at hand with complete focus, asking me lots of questions about technique, positioning, and strategy. I noticed how closely he studied our hitters to pick up tips on mechanics. In the clubhouse, we all enjoyed being around him. I smile when I think about the legendary high-stakes ping pong matches that he played against infielder Joey Cora. It's not a stretch to say that Michael treated a table tennis loss to Joey the same as he would a Game 7 defeat in the NBA Finals. That's the type of fierce competitor he was. If anybody could make it to the majors by sheer will, it was Michael.

About halfway through our spring training schedule, Michael started playing with the minor-leaguers. I'm pretty sure he realized that he hadn't improved enough to make the major league team in 1994, so he accepted the assignment without protest. In 13 exhibition games for us, he went 3-for-20. Then, with the minor-leaguers, he went 4-for-22. At the end of camp, the club sent him to our Double A team in Birmingham, Alabama, where as a first-year player, he was in line to earn $850 a month, plus $16 a day in meal money. "Right now, he's just a member of the ballclub," White Sox general manager Ron Schueler told reporters. "He'll be treated just like any other player."

I can't say that every player in the White Sox system embraced Michael's presence. There were guys fighting for roster spots who probably harbored resentment and felt he was being treated differently because of who he was. They weren't wrong, of course. Charles Poe, an outfielder in our minor league system, was the player most directly affected by Michael's assignment to Birmingham. Poe had played High A ball the season before and appeared ready to move up the ladder in '94. Then Michael came along and took his roster spot. I've read that Michael kept tabs on Poe's career, even phoning him in 1996 after the White Sox traded him away. That says a lot about Michael.

It impressed me that Michael was prepared to pay his dues down on the farm. As anybody who's ever played in the minors will tell you, it's far from glamorous. But if you've only ever flown coach class, you don't know what you're missing in the first-class cabin. After flying (and existing) for years in first class, Michael voluntarily decided to adapt to a lesser lifestyle. He had his standards, however, and apparently the Barons' team bus didn't meet them. So Michael bought the team a new $350,000 bus to drive them around the Deep South.

Michael's willingness to put himself and his reputation on the line also left an impression on me. A man of supreme confidence, he surely thought he could master baseball quickly. But in the back of his mind, he had to know that failure was a possibility. Barons manager Terry Francona, a former Expos teammate of mine, was in charge of overseeing the next phase of Michael's baseball adventure.

I'm sure Terry benefited from the experience of managing such a high-profile player.

Before Michael reported to Birmingham, he suited up as a member of the major league team for the annual Windy City Classic game between the White Sox and Cubs. In front of a packed house at Wrigley Field, Michael got two hits, including a two-run double. The next day, a columnist for the *Chicago Tribune* joked, "Don't get cocky, Michael. This wasn't major league pitching. This was Cub pitching. There's a difference." That was as close as Michael ever came to the majors, so I'm glad he experienced success that day.

With Michael down in Birmingham and the Cubs struggling to win ballgames, attention in Chicago soon refocused on our chances of getting back to the postseason, a task made somewhat easier by Major League Baseball's addition of a wild-card playoff team in each league. We had no real weaknesses, so it became more a question of plugging small holes in the lineup and keeping our best players healthy. We signed free agent Julio Franco to replace Bo as our regular designated hitter, and in his only season in Chicago, Julio ended up having one of the best seasons of his career.

As a team, we picked up where we left off, moving into first place in early May and staying at or near the top of the newly formed American League Central for the first months of the season. But then, in a bad rerun of 1981, the games suddenly stopped on August 11, this time because of a disagreement over a proposed salary cap that the owners believed would save small-market teams from financial ruin. A few years earlier, the owners had unsuccessfully tried to save money by colluding to prevent free agents from earning market value. With the Collective Bargaining

Agreement set to expire at the end of the year, a proposed salary cap represented the latest attempt by the owners to keep payrolls down.

At the time of the strike, our record stood at 67–46 and we held a one-game lead over the Cleveland Indians in the AL Central. I didn't think the strike would last very long. It was already August, and even a two- or three-week strike would create a major disruption. But both sides locked in and wouldn't budge. The head of the players union, Donald Fehr, refused to discuss any plan that included a cap on salaries, a provision that the owners considered non-negotiable.

I returned home to Florida during the strike to be with my wife and two sons, Tim Jr. and Andre. The only silver lining of the forced break was that it allowed me to perform some of the fatherly duties that I usually missed while playing a 162-game major league season. I woke up at 7:00 every weekday morning to take Andre to school, and after school, I got a chance to watch my sons play Little League. They both had a lot of talent, but at 14, Little Rock was starting to show star potential on the baseball diamond.

The weeks passed, and finally, on September 14, acting commissioner Bud Selig announced the cancellation of the rest of the season and the postseason. For the first time since 1904, there would be no World Series.

I couldn't believe it. As a longtime major-leaguer, I knew all about the realities of the business side of the sport, but I never thought the game itself would ever take such a backseat to the finances.

The statistics from that season are frozen in time. In winning his second consecutive MVP award, Frank Thomas turned in one of the best seasons in baseball history, hitting .353 with 38 home runs and 101 RBIs in just 113 games. You can still hear the bitterness in Frank's voice when he talks about being robbed of a chance of winning the Triple Crown that season. "It was very disappointing that I didn't have a chance to finish what I started," he says. "I couldn't have played better than I did that season."

In addition, we had four starting pitchers who probably would have won at least 15 games each. How strong was the rotation? Three pitchers on the staff put up better numbers than reigning Cy Young award winner Jack McDowell. I didn't have a great year, but I did enough offensively to help keep us competitive.

If a season doesn't come to an end, can you really claim you won a division title? Technically speaking, as the team that sat in first place when play stopped in '94, the White Sox captured the first-ever AL Central crown. But in reality, there were no winners in that lost season, only losers. It just so happened that the teams playing some of the best baseball that year were us and the Montreal Expos, whose record stood at 74–40 when the strike hit.

What might have happened if the season had played out to its conclusion? That question leaves a lot to the imagination. It's possible that the White Sox and Expos would have won their respective divisions and ended up meeting in the World Series. We'll never know if that would have happened. One thing's for sure, though. That potential meeting with my former team would have been the perfect scenario for me.

Some people think an appearance by the Expos in the World Series might have also saved baseball in Montreal. So much has been written on that subject that the '94 Expos have developed a certain mythology. Many baseball writers believe they were the best team in franchise history. I'm not here to argue against that claim, even though I played on some pretty good Expos teams myself. It's beyond dispute that the '94 club was loaded with talent. Moises Alou, Cliff Floyd, Marquis Grissom, and Larry Walker led an explosive offense that combined speed with power. Despite only playing until August, the Expos had seven players who reached double digits in stolen bases. The pitching staff wasn't bad either, with veteran Ken Hill and youngster Pedro Martinez anchoring the rotation. For the first time since the early 1980s, baseball became exciting again in Montreal. If the '94 team had kept winning, the course of history may very well have changed. Instead, when the strike finally ended the following spring, the Expos dismantled the team, trading Hill, Grissom, and closer John Wetteland, and letting Walker leave as a free agent.

I can't tell you how much I would have enjoyed a White Sox–Expos World Series in 1994. My new team facing my old team would have been an amazing experience. Not getting that opportunity ranks as the second-biggest disappointment of my career behind the Expos' loss to the Dodgers in the 1981 National League Championship Series.

Just for fun, and since there was nothing better to write about, the *Chicago Sun-Times* used a computer simulation to determine that season's pennant winners. The computer spit out a match-up between the White Sox and the Atlanta Braves, and it had me hitting a game-winning, extra-inning double in Game 3.

There's no telling if the computer was even close to being right. It could have been us versus the Braves, Expos, or any number of other teams. It might not even have been us. The AL Central race was tight. And the Yankees had the best record in the American League at the time of the strike. The point is, we'll never know. That's a shame.

Because of the strike, all anybody can do is speculate on what might have happened that season and down the road. A few years ago a sporting goods company created an Expos "1994 World Series" cap that it called the "What If" cap. The item sold out almost immediately. The million dollar question is whether the Expos would still be in Montreal if that season had resulted in a World Series appearance or victory. I guess you could argue that keeping the core of the team together could have resulted in a long run of playoff appearances and an ensuing revitalization of baseball in Montreal.

With the owners and the union still locked in a game of chicken by spring training, the owners decided to go forward with plans to play the 1995 season with replacement players. I thought that was crazy, but no crazier than canceling the final months of the previous season.

I didn't feel any anger toward the players who crossed the picket lines for their shot at making a major league roster. A lot of them were career minor-leaguers who were only going to make it as scabs. They had dreams to fulfill and families to provide for. Who am I to say that what they did was wrong?

The strike of '94 had so many negative consequences that it's easy to forget how it pretty much put an end to Michael Jordan's baseball career. Michael didn't set the world on fire during his time in Double A, hitting just .202 with three home runs and 51 RBIs.

He stole 30 bases, but he got caught 18 times. Michael didn't want to call it quits, however. After the minor league season ended, he went to play in the Arizona Fall League alongside some of the best prospects in the game. He raised his average by 50 points in Arizona and told everyone how excited he was to report to spring training in 1995. But when the strike lingered, Michael opted against being the richest scab in camp. Within weeks of leaving spring training, he was playing again for the Bulls. He shot 7-for-28 in his first game back, proving that even the greatest players on earth get rusty. The Bulls lost in the conference semifinals that spring before reeling off another three straight NBA championships.

ESPN showed a great documentary a few years ago titled *Jordan Rides the Bus* that documented his months in the minor leagues. What did the sports world learn from Michael's baseball experiment? The biggest takeaway, I hope, is that baseball is a difficult game to master. But with time, Michael may have actually become a solid player.

The strike finally came to an end on April 2, 1995, less than a week before replacement players were scheduled to take the field for the start of the season. As far as I could tell, the players union won the battle of wills. A salary cap never came into existence. The closest thing baseball got was a luxury tax imposed on baseball's biggest spenders. But there were no winners, really.

I reported to spring training about five pounds above my normal weight, and after a few weeks of exhibition ball, an abbreviated 144-game major league season started on April 25. I don't think the owners, or the players for that matter, realized just how angry baseball fans had become during the 232-day strike. The people who filled stadiums and supported their teams (both emotionally and financially) found themselves with absolutely no voice in the dispute that had led to the cancellation of one of the greatest American traditions, the World Series. Absence can make the heart grow fonder, but not in this case. The strike turned off a lot of fans, who showed their displeasure by avoiding major league ballparks once we returned to the field. Attendance decreased by something like 20 percent in 1995. I understood the mindset of the fans. There's nothing better on a summer night than taking in a ballgame with the family, but the strike caused many fans to shun the game for a while.

It also affected the enthusiasm level of some players. On the 20th anniversary of the start of the strike, Dave Stewart, whose lights-out performance against the White Sox in the '93 American League Championship Series earned him MVP honors, told *USA Today* that he didn't feel the same way about baseball again after the strike. He retired from the game in July 1995. He wasn't alone. Other guys at the tail end of their careers realized that they enjoyed spending time at home more than the grind of a major league season.

What kept me going? A deep and abiding love of the game, for sure, and a strong desire to play on a championship team. It was up to my teammates and me to fulfill that goal, and in the process, to win back the support of our fans. It didn't help our cause that we started the '95 campaign with four consecutive losses. The magic of the previous two seasons had vanished. So had a lot of our fans and players like Jack McDowell, who we traded to the Yankees in December 1994 for two minor-leaguers.

We committed six errors in our first win of the season, a 17–11 slugfest against the Red Sox. That performance kind of summed up our season. Even in victory, we weren't very impressive. Gene Lamont, who had won Manager of the Year just a few seasons before, got fired in early June. Schueler replaced him with third-base coach Terry Bevington. We never got higher than third place that season. Meanwhile, the Cleveland Indians reached 100 victories, despite playing only 144 games, giving them the first of five straight division titles.

Despite our poor showing, I have some positive memories of the '95 season. I got a chance to play that year with John Kruk, who had one of the greatest personalities in the game. With his roly-poly physique, John didn't look much like a ballplayer...unless the ball you're talking about is a slow-pitch softball. The greatest thing about him was that he could laugh at himself. Speaking of his stout build, he said, "Somebody said that Roseanne Barr should play my life story." In John's case, appearances were deceiving, because he could hit a baseball with the best of them. He could even run a little bit, stealing 18 bases for the Padres earlier in his career.

After signing a free-agent contract with us, John let it be known that 1995 would be his last season in the majors. He had helped lead the Phillies to the National League pennant in 1993 and wanted one last shot at playing in another World Series. When it became apparent by the end of July that he wasn't going to get that chance with the White Sox, he decided to hang up his spikes. There was just one problem: in his final games in a big league uniform, he got mired in a terrible slump that threatened to drop his career batting average below .300. He wanted to go out on a high note. So after getting a hit in his first at-bat of a July 30 game against the Baltimore Orioles, which raised his season average to .308 and guaranteed he would achieve the .300 milestone for his career, he told Lamont that he was hitting the road. He went into the clubhouse, showered, and left the ballpark. John got a lot of attention for his humorous antics, but he never sought to draw attention to himself. That's why he walked away from the game in the manner he did.

Jim Abbott is another guy I enjoyed sharing a field with in Chicago. After several seasons in California and New York, he signed with the White Sox as a free agent before the '95 season. For those of you who don't know his inspiring story, Jim was born without a right hand, and he defied the odds and went on to become a successful major league pitcher. He perfected the ability to place his glove on his right forearm while throwing a pitch and then immediately putting the glove on his left hand in case a ball got hit back to him. It was a sight to behold. Jim had some good years and some not so good years in the big leagues, but the no-hitter he threw for the Yankees in 1993 remains one of baseball's all-time great moments. When he moved to the National League at the end of his career, Abbott took some cuts at the plate and got a couple of hits. In '95, he emerged as one of our best pitchers before we traded him back to the Angels before the trade deadline.

I wasn't long for the Windy City, either. Even though I still had an option year left on my contract, my fifth season in Chicago turned out to be my last—as well as an audition for teams in the market for a player who could get on base and make things happen. In 1995, I had a .374 on-base percentage, a career-high 67 RBIs, and stole 13 bases. That made me an excellent fit for the Yankees, who desperately needed a guy who could get on base and run. No one on the Yankees had stolen more than 10 bases in 1995, and even though my years of 70-plus stolen bases appeared well behind me, I could still be counted on to put pressure on opposing defenses with my legs. On December 28, 1995, the Yankees acquired me for a player to be named later. Following the announcement of the trade, new Yankees manager Joe Torre told reporters that I would have the green light to run "99.9 percent of the time." Torre also praised my leadership and heart. I liked that show of support. And by signing me through the 1998 season, the Yankees also demonstrated their belief that I was more than just a short-term fix.

I didn't know much about Joe as a manager. I remembered him from his time leading the Braves in the 1980s, but I didn't associate his name with winning. In fact, I associated him more with broadcasting than managing. As manager of the Mets, Braves, and Cardinals, his career record wasn't much above .500, a fact pointed out by reporters critical of the hire.

Time and again during my first season playing for him, Joe had to show a thick skin when dealing with the skeptics. I had heard all about Yankees owner George Steinbrenner and his reputation for taking a very hands-on role with the team. Say what you want about George, but he was a guy who wanted to win. I think George liked that Joe was a New Yorker, born and raised. The team needed a jolt, and who better than a Brooklyn guy to provide it?

For two guys who had a history of bad-mouthing each other in the press, Steinbrenner and White Sox owner Jerry Reinsdorf had developed a fondness for making deals with each other. In response to Steinbrenner referring to him and former co-owner Eddie Einhorn as "Abbott and Costello," Reinsdorf said, "How do you know when George Steinbrenner is lying? When he moves his lips."

But that history of insults didn't stop Jerry from trading McDowell and me to the Yankees in consecutive years. By the time of my trade, Jack had already left the Bronx for Cleveland. He won 15 games in his only season with the Yankees, but his season in pinstripes is probably best remembered for the time he gave Yankee Stadium fans the middle finger for booing him. McDowell joined a lengthy list of players who didn't enjoy the spotlight of the Bronx and got run out of town. I won't judge Jack for that action. Obviously the stress of playing in New York got to him.

It remained to be seen how I would deal with the unique pressure of wearing Yankee pinstripes. From a media standpoint, no team (or company or politician) got more attention. Montreal had two main newspapers, one in French. Chicago had two prominent English-language papers. The New York metropolitan area had at least half a dozen that covered the Yankees, and each was on a mission to dig up and magnify every detail. If you weren't doing well, the fans and media let you know about it. A lot of guys over the years let that get in their heads.

I had to think long and hard about whether I felt I could thrive in the Big Apple. Ultimately, I decided that I could and I embraced the trade. The White Sox seemed intent on rebuilding without me, and Cleveland stood in the way of any AL Central team hoping to win the division. I didn't like the idea of spending the last productive years of my career with a team that couldn't get to a World Series. The Yankees knew all about winning championships, even though they hadn't done so since 1978, an epic drought by their standards. And the 1995 season had ended painfully for the Yankees. After jumping out to a 2–0 lead against the Mariners in the American

League Division Series, New York lost three straight games in Seattle. The Yankees weren't accustomed to that kind of failure.

There was a lot of uncertainty going into the '96 season. Don Mattingly had retired after 14 years in pinstripes, a rookie was penciled in as the starting shortstop, and general manager Bob Watson had to get creative to patch together a starting pitching rotation. Even the spring training site, in Tampa, was going to be new. On paper, it didn't look like the jigsaw puzzle would fit together. But thanks to a combination of youth and veteran talent, great managing, and perfect team chemistry, the small puzzle pieces resulted in an amazing big picture.

CHAPTER NINE

9

THE YANKEES HAD A LOT of new, old faces on the roster in 1996, and I was one of them, a fact that the New York media quickly seized on. In camp, reporters kept asking me a variation of the same question: do you still have it? By "it," they meant enough left in the tank to make a meaningful contribution to the team. The White Sox apparently didn't think so. Otherwise, they wouldn't have traded me *and* agreed to pick up half of my first-year salary with the Yankees.

What did the reporters expect me to say? That the White Sox were absolutely right about me being over the hill? Instead, I took the bait and offered some overly ambitious preseason predictions. I said I didn't see why I couldn't steal 40 or more bases, even though I hadn't reached that mark since 1992. When word about that comment got out, other writers flocked to my locker to follow up with me. When all was said and done, I apparently hadn't ruled out stealing *80* bases in 1996. I don't remember ever saying that, and if I did, I must have been joking. But I learned a lesson early on in spring training: you don't joke around with Yankee beat writers, who treat every player interview like an event of major international significance.

All of the spring training exaggeration aside, the Yankees were counting on me to run often, a nice contrast to the White Sox's tendency to put the brakes on me because of the slugger I had hitting behind me. I made the most of my stolen-base attempts in Chicago, at one point stealing 40 bases in a row without getting caught. I told the press that I was excited to run frequently in New York. I didn't mean it as a knock on my former team, but when White Sox general manager Ron Schueler got wind of my remarks, he fired back in the *Chicago Sun-Times*: "The thing that he says we didn't let him run was just off the wall. He had the green light the whole time. I just don't think he wanted to take the chance of getting hurt anymore." Schueler added that he thought I had "lost a lot of enthusiasm to go out there every day."

Let's just say Schueler and I didn't agree on how much I could still contribute to a team. He felt like I wasn't the same player he traded for five years earlier. And in some ways, he was right. But that didn't mean I was a liability or had lost my enthusiasm for the game. Diminished ability and passion are career-killers. It's difficult enough to overcome one of those things, but there's no way to conquer both. A lot of guys decide to retire because they look in the mirror and see someone who can no longer play at a high level, someone who isn't excited to compete anymore, or both. When I saw my reflection, I saw neither.

Although the White Sox organization and I weren't on great terms when I left, I still have overwhelmingly positive feelings about my time in Chicago. The 1993 and 1994 teams were two of the best teams I ever played for, and I remain friends to this day with former teammates like Frank Thomas and Robin Ventura. I didn't let

Schueler's comments bother me, nor did I view them as giving me added motivation to prove him wrong. I wasn't perfect, but anybody who watched me play over the course of my career knew I did so with passion. The remarks simply reinforced the notion that I had needed a change of scene.

My first game in pinstripes at Yankee Stadium took place in the snow. We're not talking about a few flakes gently falling from the April sky, either. It was a full-scale blizzard. That didn't keep 56,000 people from coming out to see Andy Pettitte gut out his second win of the young season. As a rookie in 1995, Andy had earned 12 victories, the second most on the team. Now at the age of 24, the team was counting on him to help anchor the staff. Our home opener kind of symbolized the entire season. Whatever came our way, whether it be snow, slump, or injury, we handled like winners.

The Yankees definitely featured one of the most interesting pitching rotations in baseball in 1996. There was Dwight Gooden, a former Cy Young award winner and World Series champ with the Mets who got suspended for the entire 1995 season after testing positive for cocaine. I don't think anybody knew what to expect from Dwight, including the Yankees, who signed him to a one-year deal. In his last seasons with the Mets, he didn't look anything like the pitcher who had owned National League hitters in the mid-1980s. I knew firsthand just how dominant he could be back then with his fastball and sweeping curve; in 46 career at-bats against him, I hit just .174. Dwight was only 31 years old when he joined the Yankees, but he had a lot of hard living behind him. If he could pitch effectively in '96, we'd have one less thing to worry about.

Though he didn't look sharp in his first few starts of the season, his mid-May no-hitter against the Seattle Mariners showed how good he could still be.

We were also counting on another former Met and Cy Young award winner to keep us in games. David Cone, who was in his second season with the Yankees, ended up missing most of the '96 season because of an aneurysm in his right pitching arm. Fortunately, he made it back to the field when we needed him most.

Jimmy Key and Kenny Rogers rounded out the opening day rotation. In his first two years with the Yankees, Jimmy won a total of 35 games, but he was coming off an injury that caused him to miss almost all of the '95 season. Jimmy, a lefty, was one of the few pitchers who gave me fits on the base paths. During his windup, his right leg would hang in the air, giving him the option of delivering a pitch or throwing over to first base without committing a balk. He successfully used that pickoff move against Otis Nixon in Game 4 of the 1992 World Series, helping the Blue Jays defeat the Braves.

Kenny, another guy who could pick off runners with the best of them, wore the label of "big-time free agent" before he ever pitched a game for the Yankees. Following an All-Star season with the Texas Rangers, he signed a four-year, $20 million contract with the Yankees. During spring training, one of the New York papers called the Rogers signing "one of George Steinbrenner's classic panic moves," an acquisition prompted partly by the rival Baltimore Orioles bringing in a number of high-priced free agents during the off-season. I don't recall ever reading that kind of take in a Montreal newspaper. Maybe they wrote like that in Chicago from time to time, but I'm not sure. I learned early on that being a member of the Yankees put you under a microscope. A lot of teams showed interest in Rogers after his career year in Texas, and truth be told, Steinbrenner probably overpaid to get him. I can't help but wonder, though, whether the criticism of the signing doomed him before he ever stepped onto the mound at Yankee Stadium.

With the exception of the still unproven Pettitte, yet another guy with a nasty pickoff move that bordered on a balk, I knew what all of our starting pitchers had it in them to do, but I couldn't say how it would all work out over the course of a long season. The responsibility for handling the pitching staff fell into the hands of veteran catcher Joe Girardi, who after seven seasons with the Chicago Cubs and Colorado Rockies was playing his first season in New York.

The questions surrounding how much I could contribute to the Yankees made me part of a larger narrative for the '96 season. Everyone agreed we had an interesting combination of players (a group that would become even more interesting as the season went on), but whether or not we would jell as a team remained in doubt. The Yankees were relying heavily on veteran players in '96, but they thought highly enough of 21-year-old rookie Derek Jeter to give him the starting shortstop job. The previous five seasons had featured a revolving door at the position, with Alvaro Espinoza, Andy Stankiewicz, my former Expos teammate Spike Owen, Mike Gallego, and Tony Fernandez all getting turns at short. The organization had high hopes that Jeter, a first-round draft pick in 1992, would offer some stability at the position. Well, we all know how that turned out.

But before Derek solidified his status as one of the greatest players of all time, he was a kid thrown into the pressure cooker of playing in the Bronx, touted as the next big thing. A lot of young men would have gotten crushed under the weight of such heavy expectations. Not Derek, who carried himself like a seasoned professional from the moment he stepped onto a major league field. In our first game of the season, he hit a home run and made a terrific over-the-shoulder catch that saved a run, the type of performance that immediately led to talk that Derek would win Rookie of the Year, despite there being 161 more games to play. The season was less than a week old before *Newsday* ran a column saying that Derek and his shortstop counterpart with the Mets, Rey Ordonez, were the future of baseball. Ordonez and Jeter "could make anybody nostalgic for the days of the Dodgers' Pee Wee Reese and Yanks' Phil Rizzuto," the column read. "What these two budding talents can do for the game—attract a new generation of fans and bring the old ones back—is something baseball desperately needs." The column reminded me of *The Sporting News* story about Fernando Valenzuela and me in our rookie years. Ordonez didn't quite live up to that billing, but Derek sure made that columnist look like a prophet. I got to know Derek very well during the years that we played together, and he remains one of the coolest cats around and among my favorite people in the entire world.

We got off to a quick start in '96. A 6–3 win over the Twins on April 28 put us in a first-place tie with the Baltimore Orioles, the team many people expected to challenge us for the American League East title. I wasn't as much a part of the team's early success as I would have liked to be, however. A fracture in my left thumb kept me off the field until mid-April. And then in late May, I strained my right hamstring running the bases, an injury that sidelined me for another month. Up until that point, manager Joe Torre had platooned me in left field with Gerald Williams, playing me mostly against right-handed pitchers. I took to the role. At the time I went on the disabled list, I was hitting .286 with a couple of home runs and six stolen bases in as many attempts. Torre had to do a lot of juggling of the lineup and rotation because of early season injuries. Key and Cone both went on the disabled list, as did infielders Mariano Duncan and Pat Kelly and center fielder Bernie Williams. A young catcher named Jorge Posada was called up from Triple A Columbus to take Bernie's roster spot. Jorge got just one hit in 14 at-bats that season. The best for him was yet to come.

There's never a good time to go down with an injury, but it especially frustrated me this time because I was having more fun on the baseball field than I'd had in a long time. I'm sure that had something to do with how things ended in Chicago. Thinking my career was on the downturn, the White Sox questioned my effort and cast me aside. On the flip side, the Yankees showed that they believed in me. In some ways, I felt like I did during my rookie year in Montreal, when I went out with youthful enthusiasm and proved I could thrive at the major league level.

In the circle of baseball life, I had returned to that same place, no longer a kid trying to make a name for himself, but rather an aging veteran trying to reestablish himself.

Despite all of the injuries, we managed not only to hold on to first place in the division but to extend our lead to six games at the All-Star break. The more we won, the more we started to believe.

Mariano Duncan's casual off-hand remark—"We play today. We win today. That's it"—became a battle cry for the team. (You have to picture it being said in a heavy Dominican accent to get the full effect.) Duncan helped exemplify what we were all about in '96. A career .267 hitter, he hit .340 that year.

In July, the Yankees added a couple more pieces to the puzzle. Darryl Strawberry, whose suspension for cocaine use in 1995 led to his exile to a Northern League team in St. Paul, Minnesota, fought his way back to the Yankees, hoping, like his former teammate Gooden, to stay clean and help another New York team win a championship. Then, at the end of the month, we acquired Cecil Fielder from Detroit in exchange for Ruben Sierra. By this point, our lead over Baltimore had increased to 10 games, and the front office was trying to engineer a team that would be capable of winning three postseason series. In Fielder, one of the great sluggers of the early '90s, we got a productive designated hitter and another veteran presence in the clubhouse. The addition of all of these seasoned players freed me up to let my personality shine through. If I had been the only veteran in the clubhouse, I may have felt tempted to act in a more serious manner. As it stood, I could keep things loose and let the other stars adopt a more fatherly demeanor.

For example, I never passed up an opportunity to show off my dance moves in the clubhouse, and my teammates got a real kick out of watching me go. It didn't matter what was playing on the stereo: rock, metal, pop, even country. I was on my feet dancing to all of it. To this day, Bernie Williams tells me that I had the best rhythm of anybody he ever played with. Bernie is a talented jazz guitarist who knows a thing or two about rhythm, so that compliment carries some weight.

As the end of the season neared, I confronted the reality that my team had more outfielders than places to put them. That meant I needed to perform at a higher level if I hoped to play down the stretch and in the postseason. Missing as much time as I did with the hamstring injury forced Torre to use other guys, and no one could argue with the results. Regardless of who Joe penciled into the lineup, the Yankees just kept winning. Joe took me aside in late August and told me he didn't see a way to play me every day but that he'd try to fit me in the lineup whenever he could. My age and my nagging injury fed speculation that I might not play any kind of role in September and October.

In mid-September, we hit a losing streak that shrunk our lead to 2½ games. That's when an injury to Strawberry forced Joe to get creative again by giving me the chance to play regularly. And I responded by playing some of the best baseball of my career. In a September 16 game against Toronto, I had two home runs and six RBIs. Five days later, I had another two-homer game against the Red Sox. Suddenly I looked like Mickey Mantle. Joe praised me in the papers for my sudden power surge and how I helped the team manufacture runs by being aggressive on the base paths. On a team that got contributions from so many different players in 1996, it was my turn to come up big.

As I said, the New York sports media is quick to celebrate you when you're riding high and equally fast to kick you in the stomach when you're struggling. My unexpected heroics in September silenced the critics who questioned why the Yankees had traded for me in the first place, speculating that it was because Steinbrenner was good friends with my agent at the time, Tom Reich. My performance also led to a lot of action in the postseason.

Under a lesser manager, the '96 club easily could have experienced infighting and bruised egos, a risk that exists whenever a team has more capable players than it does available positions. That's especially true in New York, where the media pounce on stories about dissension in the clubhouse. We didn't give them an opening, however. Every man on the roster knew his role, and for a lot of us, that meant accepting that Joe couldn't guarantee us playing time. If you were hot, you got to play. If you weren't, you had to wait your turn. He did great work with that team. We let him do his job, and he let us do ours, but there was never any mistaking who was in charge. I loved playing for Joe and with the guys on that team, who developed a closeness I had never experienced before and would never experience again.

On September 25, we clinched the AL East in style, scoring a season-high 19 runs in a rout of the Milwaukee Brewers at Yankee Stadium. I helped the cause with another home run. For the first time in 15 years, the Yankees were division champs. Cone, who had come back a couple of weeks earlier from his aneurysm surgery, pitched us to victory. He finished the season with a 7–2 record, but more importantly, he showed he was healthy enough to pitch in the postseason.

In a year when offenses dominated, our other veteran pitchers held their own. Rogers and Key won 12 games, and Gooden chipped in with 11. For the year, I hit .284 with 10 steals, a far cry from the goal that I had set for myself, but a reasonable number considering I played in only 59 games. Our success during the '96 season was a total team effort, but a couple of performances really stood out. Pettitte had a breakout season, winning 21 games and earning serious Cy Young consideration. How a team fares in close games depends a lot on the quality of closer it has. In John Wetteland, who saved a league-best 43 games, we had one of the most effective ninth-inning guys in the majors. John always seemed to put a guy or two on base before working out of a jam, but he rarely blew a save. We also had the best setup man in baseball, though he wouldn't stay in that role very much longer. Behind his almost unhittable cut fastball, Mariano Rivera struck out 130 batters in 107⅔ innings in his second season in the majors and his first as a full-time relief pitcher. Pettitte ended up second in Cy Young voting behind Toronto's Pat Hengten. Mariano came in third.

Jeter, who hit .314 with 10 home runs and 78 RBIs, easily won the Rookie of the Year award. Bernie Williams, Paul O'Neill, and Tino Martinez gave our lineup enough everyday pop to get the better of teams like the Orioles, who broke the single-season team home-run record in 1996. Behind all that power, the Orioles won 88 games and qualified for the postseason as the wild-card team. They drew AL Central winner Cleveland in the National League Division Series, while we got the AL West champion Texas Rangers.

I was thrilled to be back in the postseason. Our series against the Rangers got off to a rough start, however. Home runs by Juan Gonzalez, that season's American League MVP, and Dean Palmer, who also had a career year in 1996, gave the Rangers all the runs they needed in a 6–2 victory at Yankee Stadium. It was a frustrating loss because we outhit the Rangers and had runners on base all night against Texas starter John Burkett. We just couldn't come up with timely hits, which I knew from experience is a prerequisite for advancing in the postseason.

With a win under their belt and a quick start to Game 2, the Rangers didn't look like first-time playoff participants. In fact, they seemed totally unfazed by the pressure of playing a storied franchise like the Yankees in its home stadium. Gonzalez turned into a one-man wrecking crew, hitting two home runs off Pettitte in the first three innings to give the Rangers a 4–1 lead. Fortunately, Andy settled down after that, and our bullpen kept Texas at bay while we slowly chipped away at the lead. Fielder, who had homered earlier, singled home a run in the eighth to tie the score. The game remained tied in the 12th inning when the Rangers loaded the bases with two outs. Brian Boehringer got Palmer to fly out to end the threat. Jeter and I opened the bottom of the inning with a single and a walk. That created an obvious sacrifice situation for Charlie Hayes, who laid down an effective bunt that third baseman Palmer fielded and threw past first baseman Will Clark for an error that allowed Jeter to come around to score. We celebrated the post-midnight victory knowing that a loss in that game probably would have given our chances of surviving in the postseason a serious blow.

We still had our work cut out for us as the series moved to Texas. And again, we got the clutch hits we needed to steal a Game 3 victory. Ahead by a score of 2–1 entering the ninth inning, Rangers manager Johnny Oates opted to stick with starting pitcher Darren Oliver, who had handled us with ease after giving up a first-inning home run to Bernie Williams. Oates also may have had doubts about his closer, Mike Henneman, who had struggled all year. In a repeat of Game 2, Jeter and I started off the inning by getting on base, with back-to-back singles. My eight-pitch at-bat against Oliver forced Oates to pull him from the game and bring in Henneman. With runners on first and third and nobody out, Bernie Williams hit a game-tying sacrifice fly. Following a Fielder groundout that advanced me to second base, Henneman intentionally walked Tino Martinez, choosing to face Mariano Duncan instead. Mariano laced Henneman's first pitch to center field for a single that brought me around to score what turned out to be the winning run. We play today. We win today. That's it.

With momentum back on our side, we advanced to the ALCS the next night following our third straight come-from-behind victory. After falling behind early 4–0, we stormed back with six unanswered runs to finish off the Rangers. I started and got one hit each in every game of the series, scoring three times. Bernie Williams walked away as the hero of the series, helping to carry our offense with seven hits and three home runs. Bernie's long balls helped offset the damage done by Gonzalez's five home runs in the series. During a week when our starting pitching was shaky at best, our bullpen played a pivotal role in leading us to victory. Rivera, Wetteland, Jeff Nelson, David Weathers, and Graeme Lloyd combined for 18⅓ scoreless innings in the ALDS.

A few hours after we eliminated Texas, the Orioles did the same to the Indians, setting up an ALCS matchup against a team we got to know very well during the season. We had Baltimore's number in the spring and summer, but this was the fall, when records were wiped clean and the stakes increased. At the age of 35, Cal Ripken Jr. was appearing in his first postseason since 1983. General manager Pat Gillick had built an impressive team around the star shortstop.

As I mentioned earlier, the O's could hit home runs in bunches, which made them a scary opponent. They had seven players in '96 who went deep 20 or more times, a group that included Brady Anderson with 50 and Rafael Palmeiro with 39. I'll tell you more later about that group.

Anderson and Palmeiro played key roles in Game 1 of the ALCS, each hitting a home run. So did Bernie Williams and Rivera, who homered and pitched two scoreless innings of relief, respectively.

But the person whose name is most associated with that game didn't appear in uniform. He wasn't even old enough to drive a car. I'm referring to 12-year-old Jeffrey Maier, the kid in the right-field stands who made contact with Jeter's eighth-inning fly ball, pulling it over the wall for a game-tying home run. If you're an Orioles fan or anybody with a working pair of eyes, then Maier did more than just "make contact" with the ball. I remember Orioles right fielder Tony Tarasco flying into hysterics after the ball he expected to catch, or at least bounce off the wall, ended up in the stands. He pleaded his case to right-field umpire Rich Garcia, but Garcia and the rest of his crew declined to call fan interference. We were still more than 10 years away from instant replay, so much to Tarasco and the Orioles' displeasure, Jeter's first career postseason home run stood as called.

Bernie's 12th inning walk-off home run gave us a dramatic and controversial Game 1 win. We got a lucky break that evening. No doubt about it.

Not surprisingly, Maier became an instant villain in Baltimore and an immediate celebrity in New York. "There have been countless heroes in this magical mystery tour season who have helped the Yankees overcome one seemingly insurmountable deficit after another," the *New York Daily News* wrote the next day. "Mariano Rivera and Bernie Williams have topped that list all year. They certainly played their part again yesterday. But the terrific tandem and every other Yankees graciously surrendered center stage to Jeff Maier."

The lead of the *Baltimore Sun*'s game story took a different point of view: "The New York Yankees are known for developing great young players, but this is ridiculous."

At least the Baltimore writers could laugh about it. I'm not sure if the glove had been on the other hand that the journalists covering the Yankees would have found humor in the situation. I laughed when I heard a couple of years ago that the glove Maier was wearing that night got auctioned off for $22,000. The buyer chose to remain anonymous, so we don't know if the glove was destroyed by an Orioles fan or sits on the living room mantel of a Yankees fan.

To their credit, the Orioles jumped right back in the series the next afternoon, erasing an early two-run deficit and winning 5–3 to take back home-field advantage in the seven-game series. With the series shifting to Baltimore for the next three games, the Orioles had every opportunity to make people forget all about young Jeffrey. If they got hot at the right time and reeled off three wins in a row at Camden Yards, the Orioles wouldn't need to return to Yankee Stadium. That same formula applied to us, but I don't think anybody expected us to go in and take every game in Baltimore. But that's exactly what we did.

I saw only limited action in the final two games of the series due to lingering hamstring problems that I had played through for several weeks. After every game, I wrapped my entire leg and soaked in a whirlpool. I told Torre I could continue playing, but the sight of me hobbling around the clubhouse looking like a mummy didn't inspire confidence. The "next man up" mentality that had helped us win a division title played out again in the postseason. In my absence, Strawberry stepped in and stole the show, hitting two home runs in Game 4 and another in Game 5.

Against Baltimore, Bernie Williams continued his incredible postseason, with four multi-hit games. Jeter, too, got red-hot against the Orioles, going 10-for-24. They carried the offense until Darryl broke out in the final games of the series. We got two wins apiece from our starting pitchers and relievers. The Orioles hit nine home runs in five games, but our pitchers registered enough key outs and our batters got enough timely hits to win us the pennant.

I didn't realize it at the time, but until my injury took me out of action, I had a 14-game postseason hitting streak dating all the way back to "Blue Monday," the final game of the 1981 National League Championship Series. I finished my career as a .270 hitter in the postseason, but for a long stretch, I demonstrated an ability to get on base in the games that mattered most. I'm proud of that fact.

After all those years, I finally had a chance to experience a World Series, a moment I had been waiting for my whole career. It took a few days for it to sink in. I thought about Jeter, Rivera, Pettitte, and the other young guys on the team. Were they approaching their first postseason like I did back in 1981, with the assumption that win or lose, there would be many more opportunities down the line to play for a championship? I think about this question even more now in light of the success they enjoyed in the years that followed. Back in '96, nobody was using the word "dynasty" to describe the Yankees. We were simply a team battling for every postseason win, hoping that Joe put the right combination of players on the field every night.

By the time the Atlanta Braves finished off the St. Louis Cardinals in a seven-game NLCS, I was beside myself with anticipation. As difficult as it was to wait for the World Series to begin, the time off gave our injury-riddled team a chance to heal. I hoped that my hamstring could hold up for another week.

The defending champion Braves, who rallied from a 3–1 deficit to beat the Cardinals, posed a formidable challenge. In John Smoltz, Greg Maddux, and Tom Glavine, they had the best starting rotation in baseball. Braves general manager John Schuerholz saw a chance to make the rotation even better, so he acquired Denny Neagle from the Pittsburgh Pirates in late August. Smoltz, especially, was dominant in '96, winning 24 games and the National League Cy Young award.

Everyone remembers the Braves' Big Three of that era, but they were also a team that could score some runs. In '96, only the Colorado Rockies, playing in the high altitude of Coors Field, hit more home runs than Atlanta. On the rare occasions when Atlanta's pitching failed it, Fred McGriff, Chipper Jones, Ryan Klesko, and Marquis Grissom could be counted on to win games with their bats.

Game 1 of the World Series showcased the Braves at their best. In a battle of 20-game winners, Pettitte versus Smoltz, Atlanta marched into Yankee Stadium and absolutely humbled us. By the end of the third inning, Braves left fielder Andruw Jones had already homered twice to help his team race out to an 8–0 lead. Smoltz barely broke a sweat in his six innings of work, giving up two hits and one run, as the Braves went on to win 12–1.

Torre, who had kept Strawberry's hot bat in the lineup for Game 1, returned me to left field the next night. I reached base a couple of times against Maddux, but neither I nor anyone else on the Yankees crossed the plate in a 4–0 loss. Two games into the World Series, we found ourselves in a massive hole.

Following our Game 2 loss, nobody was giving us much of a chance of coming back. Jack Curry of *The New York Times* wrote that the series was over for all intents and purposes. That wasn't a minority opinion, either. Behind Smoltz and Maddux, the Braves outscored us 16–1 on our home turf. Dating back to their series against the Cardinals, the Braves were on a 48–2 run in their last five games. They looked like the team of destiny. Next up in the rotation for the Braves was Glavine, another pitcher who ranked among the best in the game. But as Girardi would later say, the '96 Yankees team had a roster full of tough-minded fighters. With the odds against us, we reached back to find one last burst of glory.

Without a day off between Games 2 and 3, we had to regroup on the fly. Another loss would pretty much kill our chances of winning the series. A win, on the other hand, would give us new life. The journalists weren't the only ones expressing doubt in us. As we prepared to take the field in Atlanta, we received a visit in the clubhouse from the Boss himself, George Steinbrenner, who told us that based on what he had seen so far we probably didn't have a chance of winning the series. "Maybe they're just better than you," he told us. "They came to New York and beat you up. I heard they have the champagne on ice already." He then encouraged us to go out there and play hard, because, who knows, anything could happen.

I had been around long enough to recognize a camouflaged motivational speech when I heard one. George hadn't resigned himself to defeat, and I'm sure the idea of losing the World Series ate him up inside. When George left the clubhouse, we got together as a team and resolved to put forth a better effort than we had in the Bronx. As clichéd as it sounded, we realized we simply needed to take it one game at a time. (Torre certainly wasn't panicking. Before our Game 2 loss, he had told the Boss not to worry; if need be, we could come back from a 2–0 hole.)

The true believers among our fan base traveled south with us. I know because I ran into a few of them in the lobby of our team hotel. The guys from Staten Island were looking for tickets to Game 3, and I happened to have a couple on hand.

Before the game, I tried to keep things light in the clubhouse, joking around with Jeter about how we needed to assemble the team's prayer group for an emergency meeting. The big smile on my face masked the nervousness I felt inside. But I thought it was important for the younger players to see a veteran player like myself acting calm and relaxed in the face of adversity.

As I walked to the batter's box to lead off Game 3, I looked out at Glavine, who was tossing his final warm-up pitches. Unlike Maddux, whose pinpoint control made it very difficult to work a walk off him, Glavine didn't possess tremendous command. I felt I needed to help set a tone for the evening by making him throw strikes. Six pitches and four balls later, I stood on first base. After

Jeter bunted me over to second, Bernie Williams singled me home to give us our first lead of the series. Cone pitched six strong innings, and we never trailed the rest of the night. Clinging to a one-run lead in the eighth, Bernie went deep for the sixth time in the postseason, hitting a two-run home run that gave us some breathing room. A 5–2 win put us right back in the series.

There was little time to savor the win, because less than 24 hours later, we were in big trouble once again, getting blown out in a game we desperately needed to have to avoid reaching the brink of elimination. After five innings of play, we trailed 6–0, and had managed just two hits off Neagle, the supposed weak link of the pitching staff. The outlook got a little brighter in the sixth when we chipped away at the lead with three runs. Still behind 6–3 in the eighth, we put together an inning that proved once and for all that October baseball doesn't have a script.

Up until that point in the postseason, Jim Leyritz had shared the catching duties with Girardi. Leyritz, a career Yankee, was a pretty decent hitter, who came into Game 4 with two career postseason home runs. But with a game on the line, he wasn't the first, second, or even eighth player on our team you'd think would play hero. That's what made his game-tying, three-run home run off Mark Wohlers so dramatic.

With two outs in the 10th in a 6–6 game, I walked to keep the inning alive. A Jeter single and an intentional walk to Williams loaded the bases for Wade Boggs, who masterfully worked a seven-pitch walk to bring me home. We tacked on another run to take a two-run lead. In the bottom half of the inning, with the tying run at the plate with two outs, Terry Pendleton lifted a fly ball to left field that kept carrying and carrying. As I slowly backed up onto the warning track, I sized up the situation and determined that the ball wouldn't leave the park or bounce off the wall. I had a play on it. What I misjudged was where I stood in relation to the wall. I thought I stood more or less flush up against it, so I shifted my weight back to use the wall for support, just in case the ball went over my head. In reality, I was a foot or two from the wall and there was nothing to keep me upright when I leaned back. As the ball came down and toward my glove, I started to lose my balance. It was a terrifying moment. Fortunately, the ball fell into my glove as I fell on my face. I rolled over and popped to my feet in one motion, trying to pass off the near disaster as an attempt at artistic flair. As I ran off the field, the grin on my face betrayed the huge sense of relief I was feeling. If I had dropped the ball, the series might have turned out differently, and my mistake would have been immortalized in the annals of postseason blunders.

That was the last time I took the field in the series. Obviously, I wish I had had the opportunity to continue playing, but time has soothed any of the bitterness I might have felt at the time toward Torre for putting Strawberry and O'Neill in the starting lineup for the remaining games, making me the odd man out. Joe's instincts had been impeccable all year, and he had earned the right to sub in players as he saw fit. At that stage in my career, I had become a role player, and my role that year was to help the team when called upon, and to wait my turn when Joe felt he had another, better option. From day one, he had hammered home the point that personal accomplishments took a backseat to team success. A lot of us weren't going to play every day. And even on days when we started a game, we had to be prepared to give way to a substitution at some point. That type of managing style isn't always going to pay off. All it takes is an alienated player or two to throw a clubhouse into turmoil. The reason it worked in our case was because we fully accepted Joe's approach.

With two straight road wins, we had climbed back into the series and guaranteed ourselves a return to New York regardless of the outcome of Game 5. We had no intention of taking our foot off the gas pedal, though. A clean sweep in Atlanta would give us tremendous momentum and leave the Braves staggering. But we had a major hurdle to get over if we hoped to go up in the series. We would be facing Smoltz, who was 9–1 in the postseason for his career, and undefeated with a 1.20 ERA in four starts in the '96 playoffs. In a rematch of Game 1, Smoltz matched up with Pettitte, who we hoped could rebound from his rough outing at Yankee Stadium.

I've talked a lot about the total team effort that led to our success in 1996. But every now and again, one of us had to carry the team on his back. In Game 5, that responsibility fell on Andy. The top of the first inning gave a clue as to what kind of night we were in for against Smoltz, who started the game by striking out the side in order. After we scored an unearned run in the fourth to break a scoreless tie, both pitchers continued to put zeroes up on the scoreboard. I watched from the bench as Andy matched Smoltz pitch for pitch, turning into a star before everyone's eyes. In the sixth, he got into his biggest jam of the night, giving up leadoff singles to Smoltz and Grissom, which prompted Braves manager Bobby Cox to call on Mark Lemke to advance the runners with a bunt. Lemke got the bunt down, but rather than take the easy out at first, Andy pounced on the ball and threw out the lead runner at third. If he had hesitated or bobbled the ball in the slightest, the bases would have been loaded with nobody out and the heart of the Braves' order coming up. But showing no signs of his youth and inexperience, Andy made the play. He then got Chipper Jones to ground into a double play to end the inning.

We didn't put up another run the rest of the night, but the Braves never got on the scoreboard. Wetteland came in to finish what Pettitte started and, just like that, we were going home needing only one win to celebrate a championship.

In order to avoid a Game 7, we needed to do more against Maddux than we had a few days earlier. We managed to get to him the second time around, plating three runs in the third inning. The Braves scored only a single run off Key, and our bullpen helped preserve a 3–1 lead going into the ninth. The Braves refused to go quietly. Wetteland gave up three hits and a run before Lemke lifted a popup that third baseman Charlie Hayes settled under in foul territory.

The play lasted only a few seconds, but it seemed like the ball hung in the air forever. In that moment, I went into another world where my baseball life flashed before me. I saw myself in an Expos uniform as a rookie competing in the playoffs. My mind went back to sitting in the White Sox dugout after coming up short in the 1993 postseason. Nothing could erase the disappointment of not winning a championship with those teams, but it filled me with satisfaction to know that my wait was about to end.

The moment Charlie caught the ball, the crowd let out a roar unlike any I had ever heard before. With Frank Sinatra's "New York,

New York" playing over the stadium loudspeakers, my teammates and I formed a dogpile near the mound. O'Neill somersaulted over all of us. Torre and his coaches embraced in the dugout. Steinbrenner and his crew celebrated from his suite. The entire team then took a victory lap around the stadium to thank the fans and share the moment with them.

I can still picture Boggs, who was also basking in the glow of his first championship, prancing around Yankee Stadium atop a police horse. He later admitted he had a fear of horses, but like all of us, he got caught up in the moment and decided to let loose. Gooden and Strawberry became the first players to win World Series as members of both the Yankees and Mets. Wetteland, who saved all four of our wins against the Braves, took home World Series MVP.

Comedian and longtime Yankees fan Billy Crystal and other luminaries joined the revelry in the clubhouse. Reggie Jackson handed the World Series trophy to Torre. It was the best party I could have ever imagined attending. Joe talked about wanting the emotions of that night to last forever, prompting Reggie, who had three World Series rings of his own, to tell him that the memories would last a lifetime.

At some point during the festivities, the emotion became too much, so I sought a quiet moment in the clubhouse bathroom. I broke down in tears, in disbelief that this had really happened. After gathering my thoughts and assuring myself I wasn't dreaming, I returned to the celebration.

The next morning, I was awakened by the ring of my home phone. It was my good friend and former Expos teammate Andre Dawson calling to congratulate me. Hawk had retired from the game a few weeks earlier, never having played in a World Series. We talked for a good while that morning. He asked me to describe how it felt to wake up a champion. I told him how lucky I was to be in the right place at the right time. As he listened, I could tell he was experiencing the moment through me.

I am proud to have been a part of such an important season in Yankees history. Bernie Williams talks about how the '96 World Series set the stage for what came later. "We wanted to be there every year, and we set the expectations high," Bernie says. "The core wasn't formed yet. That's why the veterans were so important to that team."

In 2016, I returned to Yankee Stadium for a ceremony and a weekend of festivities commemorating the 20th anniversary of the '96 World Series team. New stadium, old faces, same feeling. It was wonderful to see all of my former teammates and reminisce about that glorious season. I felt chills when I put on the Yankee pinstripes for the first time in two decades and walked out onto the field with the other players from that team. The organization didn't do much on the 10th anniversary of the '96 championship, so that weekend was the first time we were all together since that final out against the Braves was registered. I had crossed paths with a lot of my former teammates at various events over the years, including Jeter's send-off ceremony in 2014, but to all be in one place at one time celebrating a career highlight for all of us was definitely something special.

One by one, Yankees public address announcer Paul Olden introduced us to the fans. When my turn came, I jogged out to left field and slowly took in my surroundings. The first thought that popped into my head was, *I'm ready to play today.* Then reality quickly set in. At 56 years old, the drive was still there, but the same couldn't be said for my physical tools. But that was okay, because I, like Joe and everyone else associated with the '96 Yankees, had enough memories to sustain me for a lifetime.

After the hoopla ended that day, the 2016 Yankees took the field for a game against the Tampa Bay Rays. The New York lineup included two players making their major league debuts, first baseman Tyler Austin and right fielder Aaron Judge. I had barely taken my seat in the alumni suite when Austin and Judge hit back-to-back home runs in the first inning. I couldn't think of anything more appropriate than that. On a day when the Yankees organization celebrated past glory, it got a glimpse into what seems like a bright future. That's what baseball is all about.

A day rarely goes by when I don't think about that Yankees team. My mind will occasionally flash to a scene in the clubhouse where I'm joking with Jeter about his life as a bachelor. Or it might be when I'm watching TV and an old rerun of *Seinfeld* comes on that features a plot involving the Yankees teams of that era. There's the episode where Kramer promises a kid in the hospital that O'Neill will hit two home runs in a game for him, but O'Neill falls short when his second "home run" of the game is scored a triple and an error. It was nice to see Paul in a comedic role. No player smiled less or destroyed more water coolers than him.

It fills me with tremendous pride every time I hear Jeter tell reporters that he learned to have fun and enjoy the game from me. Having the opportunity to watch him in his rookie season ranks up there with the greatest experiences of my career. The '96 team was special, not only for its accomplishments, but for what it signaled for the future. I feel lucky to have had the chance to play with Jeter, Rivera, Pettitte, and Posada, the core four who would go on to lead the Yankees for the rest of the old millennium and into the new one.

CHAPTER TEN

10

ON THE BEAUTIFUL FALL DAY that I traveled down Broadway on the Yankees victory float, ticker tape dancing in the air, I felt an incredible sense of joy and satisfaction. After more than 15 years in the game, I finally knew what it was like to win it all, and the party thrown for us in New York City put an exclamation point on a magical season. Some reports estimated that more than 3 million people attended the parade, which served as a reminder that Yankees baseball had a special place in the hearts of so many fans. Everything in New York tends to be bigger and better, and the World Series celebrations are no exception.

For me, 1996 will always be synonymous with victory and completion. Prior to my arrival in New York, I had played on some teams that had a lot of talent and won a lot of games, but whether it was the 1981 Expos or the 1993 White Sox, there was always a roadblock. Under the leadership of Joe Torre, our Yankees team fought tooth and nail to get to a place I had always dreamed of being: the top of the heap.

In baseball and in life, I've never believed in cutting corners. As I said on the day in 2013 that I was inducted into the Canadian Baseball Hall of Fame, "It wasn't my intention to play the game to be the best. It was my intention to play the game to do my best." In other words, I believed in putting in the work necessary to achieve a goal so that regardless of the outcome I could look back with pride on my performance.

Unfortunately, starting around 1996, a lot of Major League Baseball players took a shortcut by using performance-enhancing drugs. Am I the best person to lecture on this subject? Probably not. As I've already acknowledged, I made some poor decisions early in my career with drugs, a result of my youth and the temptations that surrounded me.

But I didn't take the drugs because they gave me an edge on the field. I took them because I was foolish. My drug of choice, cocaine, didn't make me better, and I never would have become the player I did if I hadn't gotten my addiction under control quickly.

I realized that major league players were doing something unnatural when I started seeing baseballs flying out of stadiums at an incredible pace. Seventeen players hit 40 or more home runs in 1996, compared to just five in 1993. A lot of players and fans remember the season that Brady Anderson of the Baltimore Orioles put together in '96. I know I do, probably because I thought of leadoff hitters like Anderson as belonging to a special fraternity of baseball players. The fact that he played on the division-rival Orioles made me that much more aware of his exploits in '96. In 1995, Brady and I put up very similar power numbers. He had 16 home runs and 64 RBIs. I had 12 home runs and 67 RBIs. He stole twice as many bases as me, making him arguably the more valuable leadoff guy at that point in our respective careers.

In '96, I remained the same type of player I had always been, albeit one slowed by time and injuries. Meanwhile, in his ninth season in the majors, Brady transformed himself into a power-hitting machine. Coming into the season, he had never hit more than 21 home runs in a season. In 1996, he came out of nowhere to blast 50, the second most in the majors behind Mark McGwire. Back then, 50 home runs were a big deal, so everyone, me included, had to wonder what the heck was going on with this guy. I don't know the answer to that question. Maybe it was a fluke season.

Whatever the reason for Anderson's unexpected performance in '96, it became clear in the years that followed that something suspicious was going on in the game of baseball. A lot of guys started suddenly putting on a lot of muscle and hitting ridiculous numbers of home runs. You couldn't help but notice the bodybuilder physiques of some of these guys. And it couldn't have been all natural. Based on the sheer number of games they play, baseball players don't have as much of an opportunity as athletes in other sports to pump weights during the season.

During the peak years of my career, most teams scored runs using speed, contact hitting, and the occasional home run. In 1982, major league teams hit a total of 3,379 home runs. But that formula got flipped on its head in the steroid era, when the home run became a dominant part of the sport. In 2000, there were a record 5,693 homers hit across the big leagues. A lot of people liked the fact that baseball games became home-run derbies. Not me, though. I had nothing against the home run and always enjoyed hitting them myself, but when balls started continuously flying out of ballparks, something fundamental about the game changed.

Never in my 23-year career did I see steroids used openly in a clubhouse. But my suspicions about the prevalence of performance-enhancing drugs continued to grow in the years leading up to my retirement. The Mitchell Report on steroid use in baseball, which came out in 2007, listed a number of players, including three I played with in Baltimore—David Segui, Jerry Hairston, and Brian Roberts—in relation to banned substances. (Hairston always denied the allegations.) I should add that the report didn't mention Anderson, who was still with the Orioles in 2001.

Every player looks for a competitive advantage in the game, whether through the skills of observation or physical and mental adjustments. Too many players in the 1990s and 2000s thought they could get ahead by taking a chemical shortcut. That much is obvious to any player or fan who saw home-run records fall by the wayside. Some of the players who got caught were great players who would have been surefire Hall of Famers if they hadn't juiced. As a result of that decision, their legacies and accomplishments were tarnished. I don't feel an ounce of sympathy for those players. They cheated, and they know they cheated. By putting their own interests above those of the game, they committed acts of pure selfishness.

Major League Baseball could have done more to stem the problem earlier. Steroids had been on the banned-substances list since 1991, but the league didn't start testing for PEDs until 2003. That left a lot of time for players to basically do what they wanted with their bodies. When I look at some of the top sluggers of the late 1990s, I can't escape the likely conclusion that a good number of those players were juicing. That contributed to a rewriting of the record book and the history of the game itself.

I make all of these observations with the benefit of hindsight. At the time, I wasn't sure what was really happening or how much the problem would grow. I was too focused on my own livelihood and communicating through my performance that I had no intention of winding down my career after winning a World Series title.

During the off-season, the Yankees added yet another outfielder to the mix, bringing in free agent Mark Whiten. General manager Bob Watson made it clear at the time of that signing that Whiten would be competing with Darryl Strawberry and me for playing time in left field. Long gone were the days when I could show up to spring training with a guaranteed job. At that point of my career, I had to fight to keep my spot on the roster.

One of the New York papers described me as being at "a personal crossroads" as the Yankees decided whether to platoon me in left field, use me sparingly as a fifth outfielder, or trade me away. Obviously I wanted to stay in the Bronx to enjoy the post-championship glow with my teammates and to try and win another one. I didn't know what it was like to experience a season with a team that had just won the World Series, and I wanted to find out. On the other hand, I didn't like the idea of wasting away on the bench when I knew I could still play. Obviously, I needed to remain healthy, which at my age wasn't a given anymore. If my hamstrings or another part of my body started acting up, manager Joe Torre's decision about what to do with me would be easy.

Near the end of spring training, the Yankees went to lengths to try and trade me, but they couldn't find a team willing to pay my $1.8 million salary. Watson apparently talked to the Cincinnati Reds about taking me off their hands at no expense in exchange for two minor-leaguers. The Reds turned down the deal. Despite Watson's best efforts to unload me, I remained in New York.

Our opening day outfield consisted of Strawberry, Bernie Williams, and Paul O'Neill. Torre stuck with that formation until Strawberry went down with a knee injury five games into the season. That gave Whiten an opportunity to show what he could do in the outfield. I didn't see any action at all until our ninth game of the season, when I came off the bench to pinch-hit. My first start came two games later as Torre, now with four outfielders at his disposal, mixed and matched us, looking for the right combination. I didn't do much early on to impress Joe or anybody else, getting only four hits in my first 28 at-bats. Then, in an April 26 game against my former team, the White Sox, I had a four-hit performance that turned things around for me. By the time Darryl started a minor league rehab assignment, I was hitting over .300 and playing with a chip on my shoulder. "All in all, I've proven I can play every day," I told reporters. "But if that's not enough for people here, so be it. If I'm not what they want, I'm ready to move on."

Maybe that sounded like an ultimatum—play me or trade me—but I'm sure it was sweet music to the ears of Yankees beat writers looking for a juicy story. In reality, it was just me sticking up for myself. If my average had remained below .200, I wouldn't have made a fuss.

As it turned out, Joe didn't have to decide between Darryl and me, because Darryl's injury problems lingered, forcing him to remain on the disabled list for another couple of months. I continued to swing a hot bat for the rest of May, getting a hit in almost every game I played, causing reporters to comment on my sudden resurrection and how lucky the Yankees were for not trading me.

That's just how it is in baseball. When you're going well, the world loves you. But the tune can suddenly change if you stumble momentarily. In my case, I mean that literally.

In a June game against the Red Sox at Fenway Park, as I scored the go-ahead run in the ninth inning, I came up hobbling. I wouldn't have hurt myself if I had obeyed third-base coach Willie Randolph's stop sign as I rounded for home, but making a dash for the plate was just me trying to help my team with aggressive base running. I left the game, hoping I just had leg cramps, but that was wishful thinking. I got diagnosed with a strained right hamstring, a stubborn injury that kept me out of action until mid-August.

As a team, we looked every bit as good as we had the season before. The only difference in '97 was that we found ourselves chasing the Orioles, not the other way around. By the time I got back on the field, Strawberry still hadn't made it back, and the Yankees had released Whiten and picked up outfielder Chad Curtis. Some of the specifics had changed, but I was back in the same position as I found myself a year before, returning from injury and trying to reestablish myself as an everyday player. In my second game back, against the Royals, Joe put me in the lineup as a designated hitter. I went 4-for-5 with three RBIs, a performance I followed up with several more strong ones. I think Torre got my message: if the Yankees were going to compete for another title, I wanted to be a part of the run.

We never caught the Orioles, but by winning 96 games (four more than in '96), we qualified for the postseason as the American League wild-card team.

I finished with a .321 batting average, my best showing in a long while, albeit in a season in which I missed a lot of time. Derek

Jeter showed that his outstanding rookie season wasn't a fluke, leading the team in hits. Tino Martinez busted out with 44 home runs and 141 RBIs, the best season of his career. And Williams and O'Neill both knocked in over 100 runs. Andy Pettitte followed up his 21-win season with an 18-win campaign, and newly acquired David Wells posted 16 victories. And in his first season as a closer, Mariano Rivera saved 43 games and posted a 1.88 ERA.

I thought we had a pretty decent chance of repeating as champions. Our team was talented, hungry to win again, and battle-tested. That's a pretty good combination in the postseason. Our first-round opponent, the Cleveland Indians, were in the midst of a run in which they made five consecutive postseason appearances. If things had gone better for them in October, they and not the Yankees would have been the most celebrated team of the '90s. As it stood, however, the Indians, despite a load of talented players, just couldn't get over the top in those years.

I started every game of the American League Division Series. In Game 1, I experienced a career highlight when I hit my first and only postseason home run. My two-run homer off Eric Plunk landed in the right-field upper deck of Yankee Stadium and tied a game that we once trailed 5–0. That earned me my first curtain call as a Yankee, a moment I'll never forget. Yankees fans may remember that Jeter and O'Neill followed my homer with blasts of their own, making it the first time in postseason history that a team had hit back-to-back-to-back home runs. We won that game 8–6.

The roles got reversed in Game 2. We jumped out to an early 3–0 lead but then watched the Indians score seven unanswered runs off Pettitte to lead them to a 7–5 victory. After winning Game 3 at Jacobs Field going away, we were just a win away from another trip to the American League Championship Series. We appeared poised to take that step when we took a 2–1 lead to the eighth inning of Game 4. But single runs by the Indians in the eighth and ninth innings gave them the win and forced a decisive Game 5 in Cleveland. The Indians won that game 4–3 to advance to the ALCS against the Orioles, who they defeated before falling to the Florida Marlins in the World Series.

The Yankees' first-round elimination in 1997 tends to get lost in the shuffle of what came before and after it. But at the time, it was disappointing. We were four outs away from the ALCS and couldn't close the deal. But as I said, a hunger to win helped separate the Yankees from other teams of the era. Who knows—coming up short in '97 may have helped pave the way for the historic run that followed.

I declared for free agency after the '97 season before signing a one-year deal to remain with the Yankees. Though I wouldn't be around to see the team develop into a full-blown dynasty, I feel fortunate that I got to enjoy one more very special season in pinstripes.

One of the few downsides of being a professional athlete is sacrificing a lot of family time. Both of my sons from my first marriage were born in the summer, so I missed a lot of birthdays, not to mention the chance to see them play youth and later high school sports. In my absence, both my sons became pretty good baseball players. My younger son, Andre, who was 15 in 1998, played American Legion ball in Orlando. Though he didn't start playing baseball seriously until he was about eight, he quickly demonstrated real talent. Meanwhile, his older brother, Tim Jr., was starring on the diamond at my alma mater, Seminole High School, in Sanford, Florida. Tim Jr. was a little taller and heavier than me, but we shared the same basic build. In his senior year, he hit .380 with six home runs and 35 RBIs on a team that reached the state championship. He also stole a lot of bases. Having grown up watching me play in the majors, Little Rock decided he wanted to follow in my footsteps. He played two years of high school football before deciding to focus on baseball. I felt he had the talent to go professional, but with two decades of experience and observation under my belt, I also knew that nothing was guaranteed.

I didn't push either of my sons into baseball and tried to make sure they were exposed to as many sports as possible. Our family home in Heathrow, Florida, had basketball and tennis courts, an indoor batting cage, a putting green, and a swimming pool. To help break up the sports-oriented theme of the house, Virginia created a "pink room" with a girlish decor that included a canopy bed and antique dolls.

Andre ultimately decided to concentrate on football. He went on to play wide receiver in college and then signed with a couple of arena league teams. He stood just 5-foot-7 but he could run like the wind.

The media started following Tim Jr. around during his senior baseball season. A few months before that year's draft, *The New York Times* featured both of us on the front page of its sports section. Unlike his old man, who didn't get recruited by any colleges, Tim Jr. garnered a lot of interest from top-flight college programs, including the University of Florida, to whom he orally committed pending the outcome of the draft. We hoped he'd get picked in the fourth round or earlier, but regardless of what happened, I could tell he was serious about turning professional right away.

I left the decision about his immediate future up to him. There was no right or wrong choice. He could go to college and get more experience that might improve his skills and draft stock. Or, if drafted, he could take advantage of the opportunity that presented itself and turn pro. He had to do what his heart was telling him. I didn't want him to feel pressured to take the path I had chosen for myself. After all, without any offers to play college baseball, my choice was pretty much made for me. He had more options.

In June, the Baltimore Orioles selected Little Rock in the sixth round of the amateur draft, a round later than I had been picked back in 1977, a fact I still kid him about it. He decided to sign with the Orioles, a decision I supported. As fate would have it, I arrived in Baltimore for a series against the Orioles on the day that my son signed his first professional contract. That definitely helped make up for not being able to attend many of his high school games. "It's a good day for the Raines family," I said at a press conference that day. "I hope I can stay up here long enough to play with him."

I knew that the odds of that happening were slim. It would require me to keep playing into my forties, and it was a long way from Tim Jr.'s first professional stop in the Gulf Coast League to the major leagues. In addition to the normal challenges facing any minor-leaguer trying to work his way up the ladder, my son also would have to confront the added pressure of having a famous father. Tim Jr. and I talked about our shared dream of playing together in the majors, but it was usually in a joking way. "I'm an old man," I'd tell him, "but I'll wait for you even if they have to roll me out onto the field when you get there."

As my older son set out on his professional baseball journey in Sarasota, the same place I reported for rookie ball two decades earlier, I continued mine on a team that was setting new standards for excellence, a real accomplishment considering the incredible track record of the Yankees franchise over the years. We entered that June series against the Orioles with a record of 47–14. And I had helped contribute to the team's success, maintaining a batting average at or above .300 for most of the season while playing on a regular basis, either in left field or as the designated hitter.

The '98 team had an ideal mix of players. Our core group from the previous seasons remained, and with a little more experience under their belts, the younger guys had become that much better. But you don't win 114 games like we did without contributions from unexpected places. I'm thinking of third baseman Scott Brosius when I say that. Scott joined the Yankees after the '97 season as a player to be named later in a deal that sent Kenny Rogers to the Oakland A's. It wasn't a marquee pick-up by any stretch of the imagination. Scott's six seasons in Oakland had been inconsistent at best, and he was coming off a year in which he finished dead last in the majors in batting average. But we needed someone to replace the departing Wade Boggs and Charlie Hayes at third, and general manager Bob Watson, who was a few months away from being replaced by Brian Cashman, thought Brosius was worth a risk. Brosius came to New York and became an overnight star. In addition to playing great defense, Scott had a career season in which he hit .300 with 19 home runs and 98 RBIs. As we soon found out, however, Scott was saving his best for last.

Certain games from that season stand out for me, like the May game against the Orioles in which Baltimore reliever Armando Benitez drilled Tino Martinez in the back with a pitch, causing a benches-clearing brawl that featured a lot of anger and punches. At one point, the action even spilled into the Orioles dugout. I think Benitez hit Tino out of frustration after giving up a three-run homer to Bernie Williams that put us up in a game we had once trailed 5–1. After order was finally restored, I came to the plate and hit the first pitch I saw into the right-field bleachers to help seal the victory. That felt good. Then there was the late June interleague contest against the Atlanta Braves, who were almost as hot as we were, causing a lot of people to call the series a World Series preview. In the first game of the set, I doubled off Greg Maddux and came around to score, and then later in the game stroked a two-run, game-winning double.

We finished the season on a seven-game winning streak, but if we didn't run the gauntlet in the postseason, we'd have nothing to show for our efforts. The ability to win games when they counted most is what separated the late '90s Yankees teams from a lot of other talent-laden clubs over the years. A team that breezes through the regular season isn't necessarily well equipped to deal with a losing streak in the postseason. And the inability to deal with setbacks can be fatal in a short postseason series.

In the 14 full seasons played from 1991 to 2005, the Braves took home 14 straight division titles, but they only won the World Series once during that span. In '98, almost everyone expected us to meet up with Atlanta in a rematch of the '96 World Series. Then, Atlanta, which won 106 games during the season, fell in the National League Championship Series to the San Diego Padres.

We ripped through the American League Division Series, sweeping the Texas Rangers in three games. That earned us another crack at the Indians. We fell behind in the series two games to one, which gave us our first real taste of adversity since the previous fall. Three straight wins later, we had a date set with the Padres in the World Series.

By this time, Torre had even more options in left field, including Rickey Ledee, Chad Curtis, and rookie Shane Spencer. Ledee ended up getting most of the playing time in the World Series, and I had to settle for watching the festivities from the bench.

I don't think anything was going to stop the Yankees from winning another championship in 1998, and the Padres didn't put up much resistance. With eventual World Series MVP Brosius leading the way with eight hits, including two home runs, we made quick work of San Diego. On a warm October night in Southern California, we put the finishing touches on a sweep. A second championship in three years reignited talk of a dynasty.

The Yankees went on to win two more World Series in a row, giving them four titles in five years, an incredible accomplishment in the age of free agency and wild-card postseason berths. Unfortunately, I didn't get to stay for the duration of that great run. In December 1998, the Yankees declined to make me an arbitration offer. That prevented me from re-signing with them until May 1 of the following season and put the wheels in motion for me to sign elsewhere as a free agent. This turn of events forced me to take a long look in the mirror. A few days before the Yankees decided I wasn't a part of their short-term plans, I had arthroscopic surgery on my left knee to help alleviate the tendonitis I had experienced near the end of the season.

I didn't have much left on my baseball bucket list. The two World Series wins with the Yankees had helped me scratch a nearly 20-year-old itch and eased the sting of being the only member of the '98 team not to be re-signed. I never played the game to accumulate personal statistics, so the prospect of a few more stolen bases didn't provide me with a compelling reason to stick around either.

No, my motivation to keep playing was twofold: first and foremost, I loved the game and couldn't imagine giving it up while I still had something left to contribute to a team. And secondly, I really did hope to play in the majors at the same time as my son. In his first year in the minors, Little Rock stole 37 bases in 41 attempts, but he still had a ways to go as a hitter. There was no telling if he would make the majors anytime soon, or even at all.

I took some time to weigh my options. For a couple of days, it looked like the Expos might be interested in bringing me back. Ultimately, that deal didn't go through. That's when the Oakland A's called with an offer.

CHAPTER ELEVEN

11

EVER SINCE MY ROOKIE SEASON, I had heard myself compared to all-time stolen-base leader Rickey Henderson. And by signing with Oakland before the 1999 season, I guaranteed myself at least another round of Rickey talk.

It made sense, because I was going to the town where Rickey had spent many of the best years of his career, most recently a year earlier when, at the age of 39, he led the American League with 66 stolen bases. Rickey left Oakland (for the fourth time in his career) before the '99 season to sign as a free agent with the Mets. In need of a left fielder, the A's decided to take a chance on me. In late January 1999, I signed a one-year, $600,000 deal with the club.

As the Oakland beat writers observed upon my arrival, I hadn't stolen more than 20 bases in five years. But A's general manager Billy Beane liked that I still demonstrated an ability to get on base consistently. At the press conference that Beane called to announce my signing, he also introduced the hiring of a young assistant GM named Paul DePodesta. The "Moneyball" era had begun.

The longer you play, the more new faces you see every season, as the old ones you got to know as teammates and opponents start leaving the game in growing numbers. The '99 A's team had some young players like Eric Chavez and Ben Grieve who were still in diapers when I broke into the majors in 1979. Talk about feeling old! That's why I enjoyed being reunited in Oakland with Tony Phillips, a guy I first met in my second year in the Expos minor league system. Tony and I had never played on the same major league team before. We had missed each other in Chicago by five days in 1996, a week that saw me sign with the Yankees and Tony sign with the White Sox. A's manager Art Howe hoped Tony and I could provide veteran leadership to a young team, along with whatever else we had left in our bats and gloves. I entered the season with a healthy dose of optimism. "I feel like I can play every day," I told reporters a couple of days after joining the A's. "I feel good and my legs are steady. I think now that since I'm healthy, I can be more of a force on the base paths."

Even in my 20th season, I was experiencing new things, like spring training in Arizona, a state I had never before visited. I arrived to A's camp three days early, joking to reporters that I showed up well ahead of time because I was afraid I might get lost on the way. My heart was still in New York, but I didn't mind going to a team in rebuilding mode. A few years earlier, when I was still in search of my first championship, that would have been a no-go, but my two World Series with the Yankees freed me up to sign with a team that would give me the most opportunities to play. The A's had a diverse mix of players competing for starting spots. There were young guys and old guys and pretty much nothing in between. I, as always, was "Rock," but my listening skills got tested when Phillips, one of the loudest and most talkative guys I ever played with, bestowed Chavez with the nickname "Rook."

In my first home game in the Bay Area, an early April exhibition against the San Francisco Giants, I hit a home run. As luck would have it, we opened the season at Network Associates Coliseum against the Yankees. It felt good to see all of my former teammates but a little strange to be playing against and not with them.

I hit safely in four of my first five games before going into one of the most prolonged batting slumps of my career. At the All-Star break, I was hitting just .218 with three stolen bases. I hoped for a resurgence in the second half of the season, but over the break I came down with an illness that left me fatigued and bloated. I must have put on 15 pounds that week, but I didn't think anything of it, assuming I had some kind of virus that would eventually just go away.

I realized something was really wrong with me on a mid-July weekend when Howe gave me a rare opportunity to start back-to-back games. By this time, my glands and ankles were swelling like crazy. I could barely keep my eyes open and had ballooned up to close to 250 pounds. Still, I felt like I could power through whatever ailed me, even though the simple act of jogging out from the home dugout to left field in the first inning left me seriously winded. I didn't want to take myself out of the game, so I completed the inning and two more after that, praying the whole time that I wouldn't have to chase down a fly ball. By the start of the fourth inning, I could no longer pretend that I was in any condition to play. "I don't think I can go," I told Howe, explaining my symptoms. That earned me an immediate trip to the hospital, where tests showed I had kidney inflammation.

The doctor performed a biopsy, and a couple of weeks later, the results came back showing I had something called lupus. I had no idea what lupus was, other than the name of a character in *The Bad News Bears*. But I quickly learned all about it. Lupus is a chronic inflammatory disease that basically results in the body becoming allergic to itself. In my case, lupus had caused my body to attack my kidneys. The scariest part of the diagnosis was that there was no known cure for the disease. "No known cure" are words you never want to hear, believe me.

Scared and a little bit stunned, I tried to make sense of what was happening. Women, especially African American women, are at greater risk for lupus, but it can strike anyone at any time. As a professional athlete, you come to think of yourself as almost invincible. Sure, you get hurt, but the occasional pulled muscle and broken bone always heal. You never think you'll be sidelined by a disease. Panic set in for a while. I didn't know if lupus would end my career or even kill me. I was relieved to learn that most people who come down with lupus get treatment and end up leading normal lives. As I prepared to turn 40, all I could do was try to bring the symptoms under control with medication and then see how it affected my ability to play baseball.

This wasn't something I ever expected to happen to me, but life throws you curveballs sometimes. Due to my illness, I could kiss the 1999 season good-bye. What happened after that remained to be seen. I made it clear to anyone who asked that I intended to return for the 2000 season, but that goal hinged on my disease remaining in remission. It was a frightening time to say the least. As I said at a press conference after the diagnosis, "As baseball players, we kind of live a sheltered life, good, bad, or ugly. I mean, you're on top of the world. You feel like nothing can ever get to you." The A's organization showed its support for me by inscribing my uniform number, 30, on every player's cap.

I couldn't play the game, but I could still bask in the memory of winning a championship the year before. In late August, I returned to Yankee Stadium with the A's to collect my 1998 World Series ring. A crowd of reporters circled me to ask about my ailment. By this time, I was starting to lose weight and barely had enough strength to stand. My agent, Randy Grossman, accompanied me because I couldn't get around on my own. It meant the world to me when Yankees manager Joe Torre came to home plate carrying a box containing my ring. When I opened the box, however, I saw that it was empty. My face broke out in a huge smile. So did Joe's. The guys were getting revenge on me for the practical jokes I had played on them. A moment later, Bernie Williams, who had come up with the idea for the prank, ran over and presented me with the ring. The entire team then gathered around me as the Yankee Stadium crowd gave me a standing ovation. That experience did wonders for my state of mind, considering how lupus had forced me to confront not only the potential end of my career but mortality in general.

For a period of time, my doctors treated my lupus like it was cancer, giving me weekly doses of chemotherapy. As anybody who's undergone these treatments knows, they take a lot out of you, physically, mentally, and emotionally. I've always considered myself a carefree, happy-go-lucky guy, but I couldn't avoid feeling really depressed during those difficult months. Prednisone, the medical steroid I took as part of my treatment, caused my mind and body to play tricks on me. I couldn't sleep, and when I did, I had terrible dreams. At times I fell into an almost zombie-like state, oblivious to everything going on around me. Other times I would fly into fits of rage. I hadn't experienced that type of moodiness since I beat my cocaine habit in the early 1980s.

During that difficult period, my mind raced all over the place. One day, while sitting at home, I burst into tears at the memory of my four-year-old sister, Anita Gail. I had long ago come to terms with the tragedy that occurred that day in 1968, but in my current state, it was if I was experiencing it all again for the first time. "I just realized my sister is dead," I told my wife, who also started crying. She had never seen me in such a vulnerable state before.

As I slowly got better, I vowed to do everything in my power to be ready for spring training in 2000. Not many players get a chance to play in four different decades, and I wanted to be one of them, especially after what I had been through. "I'm going to play again," I announced on the night I got my ring at Yankee Stadium. "Next year in spring training, I'll be with somebody. Who knows, I might be playing every day." Please keep in mind that I was heavily medicated at the time. During my trip to New York, I met with George Steinbrenner in his office. I rambled on to George about my plan to rejoin the Yankees. "As a coach?" he asked, smiling.

The Yankees won another World Series in 1999, sweeping the Atlanta Braves. In November, I became a free agent and worked out during the off-season with my son, Tim Jr., who had just finished his second year of pro ball, to get myself back into baseball shape. My chances of playing every day with the Yankees were non-existent, but *any* chance to rejoin my former team excited me. In January 2000, I had my last major lupus treatment. A month later, with my symptoms mostly in check, I signed a minor league deal with the Yankees. George obviously believed I wasn't ready to become a coach quite yet.

I had never had so much riding on a spring training performance. A strong showing would help earn me a spot on the major league roster as a reserve outfielder or designated hitter, while poor results would put a quick end to my comeback attempt. The Yankees didn't become the Yankees by signing charity cases, after all. I had to prove I could still contribute as I battled with Ricky Ledee, Shane Spencer, and Roberto Kelly for a spot in the outfield, and with Darryl Strawberry and Jim Leyritz for playing time at designated hitter. As Torre said at the time, "If I was a fan, I'd be pulling for him, but you've got to make a decision about whether you're going to be better with him or not."

The competition became less intense when Darryl received a one-year suspension in late February after testing positive for cocaine for the third time in his career. I hated to see that happen to Darryl, who I considered a very good friend. As Straw was packing up his stuff in Tampa, I took him aside to let him know I was there for him if he ever needed to talk. I could identify with what he was experiencing, not only because of my own battles with drugs, but also because he had recently dealt with a serious medical problem, beating colon cancer in 1999. As he underwent chemotherapy, he sunk into a depression that may have led him back to drugs. On the verge of turning 38 and forced to step away from the game for a year, Darryl never came back, putting an end to the career of a guy who could have been one of the all-time greats if he had conquered his demons.

I didn't play badly in spring training, but I also didn't do a whole lot to move myself up the depth chart. Torre respected me too much to mislead me into thinking I had a chance of making the club. During the middle of the exhibition schedule, he took me aside to let me know I wouldn't be traveling north with the Yankees. The news stung and forced me to confront the reality that I had probably reached the end of the road. The idea of going to the minors and trying to work my way back up didn't appeal to me. My heart was telling me I could still play, but I decided to listen to my head and started telling my Yankees teammates that I planned to retire. Then I let the world know, announcing my retirement at a press conference before a Yankees–Red Sox spring training game. "I guess we all have an alarm for when it's time for your career to end, and I felt like my alarm went off two weeks ago," I told the gathered reporters.

Later that day, I sat in the stands in Sarasota watching my 20-year-old son play for an Orioles farm team, my dream of sharing a field with him apparently out of reach. But I took comfort in knowing that I could make up for lost time by taking in as many of his games as possible. Little Rock went 1-for-4 that afternoon and made a couple of nice grabs in the outfield. The idea of being a spectator would take some getting used to, but as I sat in the Florida sun like so many retirees, I convinced myself I wouldn't miss playing.

But I was kidding myself.

In the days that followed, all I could think about was getting back onto the field. I waited for the urge to subside, but it never did. Not that there was much I could do about it. The season had already started, and it might have been difficult to secure even a minor league assignment at that point.

I huddled with Randy, my agent, to discuss the situation and then returned home to further gather my thoughts. That's when I got a call from Bob Watson, who had served as Yankees general manager for part of my time with the club. Bob had become head of the selection committee for the United States Olympic baseball team, which for the first time, was permitted to have professional players on its roster. Because the Olympics took place during the heart of the major league pennant race, no players on MLB rosters could participate, however.

For more than 20 years, I had other things going on in the month of September. But in 2000, my calendar looked wide open. Randy and I decided that this was the perfect opportunity to write another chapter in my career. No American player to that point had won an Olympic gold medal and a World Series ring—not surprising considering no American team had ever won a gold medal and no World Series–winning player had ever competed for the national team.

Watson asked me if I thought I had anything left in the tank. Hoping my confidence would help offset any shortcomings in my game, I assured him I most definitely did. Then he made an unusual request: report to an Independent League team in Bridgewater, New Jersey, for what amounted to a four-game audition for the Olympic team. I was intrigued enough by the possibility to take Bob up on his offer, and my performance with the Somerset Patriots impressed him enough to keep me in the mix for one of the 24 spots on the team. Other former major-leaguers, including my former Yankee teammate Pat Kelly and catchers Terry Steinbach and Pat Borders, were also competing to make the roster. I survived a couple of rounds of cuts until I was one of the last former big-leaguers still in consideration for a spot on the team.

The articles about my attempt to make the U.S. national team referenced my accomplishments in the past tense, portraying me as a former major-leaguer hoping to achieve Olympic glory as his last hurrah. It's true that I saw the Sydney games as a wonderful opportunity to represent my country, but I also viewed the Olympics as a chance to show major league teams that I still had enough in me to play another couple of seasons.

When it looked like I had all but sealed a spot on the team, I went back to Somerset for a few more tune-up games. Then Team USA manager Tommy Lasorda delivered some terrible news, announcing at a press conference that I didn't make the team and that he was taking a team comprised largely of unknowns to Australia. Lasorda believed that the presence of a former major league star on the roster would be a distraction. He commented at the time that he wanted players on his team to be known for the name on the front of their jersey, not on the back.

I didn't take the news particularly well.

"I wasn't the one who called them," I said after getting cut. "They called me. To take a person of my stature with the years I've put in and string me out that way, it isn't right. I don't hold grudges, but I'm upset."

After announcing the roster, Watson rubbed salt in the wound by saying, "We thanked those older guys for cranking it up again, but there's a reason they retired." Ouch.

Team USA won the gold medal in Sydney, but the way Lasorda and Watson handled the whole situation still burns me. In a way, though, I should be thankful for their decision, because it gave me even more motivation to show people that I could still play.

I returned to New York that October for the Subway Series between the Yankees and Mets. In addition to doing some television work for ESPN, I also got a chance to visit with my former Yankees teammates, who went on to win their fourth World Series in five years. Being around that celebration further fueled my desire to see if I could get myself in shape for spring training.

I didn't take the task lightly. The last thing I wanted was to fall flat on my face and have to crawl back into retirement. There's something to be said for leaving the game gracefully. If my comeback failed, a lot of people would have legitimate reason to question my judgment.

There was another key question that needed answering. I wanted to play, but did any teams have interest in me? I had planted the seed with the Expos during a visit to Montreal near the end of the season for my induction into the Expos' Hall of Fame, telling manager Felipe Alou to keep me in mind. Apparently he did, because a few days before Christmas, I signed a minor league deal with the Expos.

I couldn't have been happier. A disease wasn't going to end my career. Neither was a poor decision by an Olympic committee. I had a chance to go out on my own terms in a city where all my dreams first came true, and I wasn't going to blow it.

CHAPTER TWELVE

12

FOR ME, IT WAS THE Expos, part *deux*.

I worked my butt off in the months before the 2001 season. Never much of an early riser, I set my alarm clock for 6:00 AM so that I could get in two full workouts every day. I wanted to report for duty in top shape so that I could make a good impression on my teammates and Expos management. I looked at the upcoming spring training schedule and noticed that the Expos were scheduled to play the Orioles in early March. The possibility of playing against my son, Tim Jr., gave me even more motivation to be ready.

After three years in the Baltimore Orioles organization, Little Rock had demonstrated the ability to steal bases at the major league level. In the Carolina League in 2000, he swiped 81 bags in 127 games. His hitting still needed work, however. He had yet to hit above .250 in the minors, striking out more than a hundred times in two of his three seasons. On the positive side, he also drew a fair number of walks. If he could put the ball in play more, he'd have an opportunity to use his legs to beat out hits, which would bump his average up considerably. That was the main challenge he faced as he prepared to make the jump from High A ball to the upper minor leagues in his fourth season of professional ball.

In 2001, Tim Jr. reported to Orioles camp in Fort Lauderdale, while I began my second stint with the Expos in Jupiter. By the time our paths crossed at the spring training game, Tim Jr. had already been sent to minor league camp, but the Orioles postponed that assignment to give us a chance to play against each other. We both started and hit leadoff that day as my wife and father looked on from the stands. I got two hits. Little Rock got one. And I walked away with our lineup card as a souvenir. I didn't know if we'd ever get a chance to play with or against each other in a regular season game, so I savored the experience.

Despite feeling the rust of not having played in a major league setting in a year, I hit over .400 during spring training, dispelling any notion that the Expos would keep me around as a novelty or simply to mentor younger players on a club that had lost 95 games the season before. Shortly before the Expos were scheduled to go north, I got a visit from general manager Jim Beattie, who informed me I had made the team's opening day roster. "I didn't know whether to hug him, kiss him, or shake his hand," I told reporters. "I didn't want to holler in the clubhouse, but I felt like I was a rookie again. I felt like I was 20."

We opened the season with three games in Chicago. Against the Cubs, manager Felipe Alou opted to go with Milton Bradley and Geoff Blum in left field, limiting me to two pinch-hitting appearances during the series. That gave me a chance to re-acclimate myself to the big league atmosphere before returning to Montreal for our home opener.

I had never felt such anticipation about a game before. Eleven years had passed since I last wore an Expos uniform. A lot had changed since then. There wasn't a familiar face in the clubhouse, and the atmosphere surrounding the team had also darkened. Baseball had reached its peak of popularity during my time in Montreal, but now the Expos were struggling to fill seats. The attendance problem had grown so severe that there was talk that 2001 could be the team's last year in Montreal.

I'll never forget my first game back at Olympic Stadium, a Friday night matchup against the Mets. In the days leading up the game, reporters asked Alou whether he planned on starting me in the home opener. He wouldn't commit to it, but I think he and everyone else knew what the fans expected. And when it came time to fill out the lineup card, my name appeared as the left fielder and sixth-hole hitter.

When I was announced over the loudspeakers prior to the start of the game, the crowd gave me a long ovation. But that was only the beginning. As I approached the batter's box with two on and nobody out in the second inning, the fans again rose to their feet and let out a deafening roar. I don't know how long the standing ovation lasted, but it must have been quite a while, because Mets third baseman Robin Ventura, a former White Sox teammate of mine, signaled to me that the crowd would quiet down if I tipped my helmet to them. That may have been the case, but I wasn't really in any hurry for them to stop cheering. Up in the stands, Virginia was so overcome by the moment that she broke down in tears. I had to catch myself from doing the same. I acknowledged the fans and stepped into the batter's box against Glendon Rusch, who promptly walked me on four pitches. We scored three runs that inning and went on to win 10–6. More than 45,000 people turned out for our home opener, about six times the number we would average that season.

The team got off to a surprisingly strong start, winning six of its first seven games, but that didn't help put bodies in seats. In contrast to the electric atmosphere of the opener, Olympic Stadium felt like a ghost town on most nights.

I eventually settled back into a comfortable routine with the Expos, starting some games, pinch-hitting in others, and occasionally just watching from the bench. I didn't have much pop left in my bat or juice in my legs, but I could still get on base pretty steadily. In early May, my on-base percentage was over .400. Then in a game against Arizona, my feel-good story took a negative turn. While attempting to beat out a hit, I demonstrated that old habits die hard by diving headfirst into first base, jamming my left shoulder. I went on the disabled list and waited for the injury to heal, but an MRI revealed I had torn a muscle in my left biceps.

The injury required surgery that threatened to shut me down for the rest of the season. The rest of the season…or forever? That's what the solemn-faced reporters wanted to know, even if most were too polite to come right out and ask. By this point, they had probably lost count of the number of comebacks I had mounted. Fortunately, I knew the routine by now and had no problem confronting the question again. So just as I had after my lupus diagnosis, my release by the Yankees, and my failed attempt to make the U.S. national team, I stuck to the same line, channeling Arnold Schwarzenegger (without the accent) and telling anyone who would listen, "I'll be back."

There was no room for negativity at this point. If I had hung my head and resigned myself to once and for all calling it quits, I wouldn't have had a chance of beating the odds and returning to the Expos. So at the end of May, I underwent arthroscopic surgery on my shoulder. All I could do after the operation was wait and see how quickly I healed. My body cooperated, paving the way for a minor league rehabilitation assignment in August that included a second face-off with Tim Jr., who had cut back on his strikeouts and boosted his average, a development that led to his rapid ascension through the Orioles farm system. Our teams split a doubleheader, but that day will go down in history as the first time a father and son competed against each other in a professional regular season baseball game. Of course, my son and I had designs on sharing a major league field together.

In late August, I returned to the Expos. During my absence, the team had struggled so badly that owner Jeffrey Loria replaced Alou, the winningest manager in Expos history, with Jeff Torborg. With the team far out of contention, my top priorities for the remainder of the season were to remain healthy and to see my son get promoted to the majors. I accomplished the first goal and played pretty good baseball along the way. When I went on the disabled list in May, I was hitting .265. By early October, I had lifted my average to .308. The Orioles took care of the rest by calling up Little Rock.

My wife and I flew to Baltimore to watch our son make his major league debut. She went crazy, hooting and hollering like the proud mother she was when he entered the game as a defensive substitution that night. I tried to stay cool, remaining in my seat with a huge smile on my face while shaking the hands of everyone sitting around me. Afterward, I flew to Miami to join my team for a game against the Marlins.

Little did I know that the ninth-inning walk I received the next night would be my last plate appearance as an Expo.

Beattie knew how much seeing my son in the big leagues meant to me. I had talked publicly for years about how I wanted to stick around long enough to play at the same time as Tim Jr. It never really occurred to me that we would ever have an opportunity to play on the same team. As a veteran in decline, I didn't have the kind of pull to make that arrangement happen. But Beattie had the resolve to do it for me. He got on the phone with Orioles general manager Syd Thrift to see if they could work something out. Jim hadn't talked to Expos ownership about the plan because he first wanted to see if Thrift was on board with bringing my son and me together for the final games of the season, which had been extended an extra week into October because of the games that were postponed after the 9/11 terrorist attacks. Thrift embraced the idea, too. His team was suffering through a miserable season and had lost several outfielders to injury. Plus, he realized his fans needed something to feel good about.

When Jim came to tell me that he had orchestrated my trade to Baltimore for a player to be named later, I thought he was kidding around. He assured me he wasn't. Still, I waited to say anything to my wife, parents, and son, because I didn't want them to be disappointed in case the deal somehow fell through. I boarded a flight to Baltimore and arrived at Camden Yards as the Orioles were participating in pregame warm-ups. The clubhouse guys were really on the ball and had a uniform ready for me. I suited up and ran onto the field. When my son saw me running toward him, he looked like he had seen a ghost. He remained speechless as I went up and stood beside him. "What's up, son?" I asked matter of factly before giving him a massive hug. "Oh my god!" he repeated again

232

and again. I'm sure it was the greatest surprise of his life, and I'm so grateful that the Expos and Orioles made it possible. We stood next to each other during the national anthem that night. I'm not a guy who sheds many tears, but after everything I had experienced the previous couple of years, not to mention what the country was going through at the time, I couldn't help but get emotional. With Tim Jr. batting leadoff and playing center field that night, manager Mike Hargrove inserted me into the game as a pinch hitter in the seventh inning. That made it official: my son and I had become the only father-son duo other than Ken Griffey Sr. and Ken Griffey Jr. to be major league teammates.

The real payoff came in my second game with the Orioles, when Hargrove started us both in the outfield, him in center and me in left. The last time we had played on the same team together was during one of the annual father-son games in Montreal. Before the game, I let him know that he needed to cover a lot of ground in the outfield. "Don't make me run to my left," I told him. He smiled and told me he had my back.

I looked over at him in the top of the first inning and saw that my eight-year-old son had become a grown man. It took me several moments to gain my composure and remember I had a job to do. After Little Rock singled, stole a base, and scored in the first inning, I went over with the rest of my teammates and gave him a fist bump. I didn't want him to view me any differently from the other guys on the team, but I couldn't resist getting in a little fatherly affection. "I'm proud of you, son," I whispered to him.

Those final games of the 2001 season meant the world to me. Not only did I fulfill the dream of sharing a major league field with my son, but I also got a chance to play with Cal Ripken Jr. in his final games before retirement. I obviously didn't get a chance to know Cal very well during that week, but being able to call myself his teammate for even a short while is something I'll always cherish. I also hit my first major league home run in over two years, a shot off knuckleballer Tim Wakefield in my last start of the season.

I didn't have anything left to prove or accomplish, but I still couldn't bring myself to step away from the game. I got three hits in my last start and felt I could still help a team in need of a reserve outfielder and pinch hitter. My counterpart, Rickey Henderson, was still playing into his forties, and I drew inspiration from him to keep going. If at all possible, I wanted to experience an injury-free final season in the majors. There was no guarantee that Tim Jr. would start the 2002 season in the majors, so I didn't feel obligated to stay in Baltimore. I would have liked to go back to Montreal, but the Expos' future seemed as uncertain as ever, with owner Jeffrey Loria selling the team to Major League Baseball.

Loria used the proceeds of the sale to buy the Florida Marlins, who hired Torborg and his entire coaching staff. That made the Marlins a natural fit for me. In February 2002, I signed a minor league contract with the club, similar to the ones that I signed with the Yankees in 2000 and the Expos in 2001. If I played well enough to earn a major league roster spot, I would stick around for one more season. But if I didn't make the Marlins, I'd once and for all retire, with no regrets whatsoever.

When I broke into the majors back in 1979, Expos coach Steve Boros helped teach me the ins and outs of base running. I remember thinking at the time, *Man, this old guy really knows his stuff.* Steve was 42. In 2002, when I worked with Marlins second baseman Luis Castillo on his stolen-base skills, so was I. That made me the old guy, but I was happy to take on the role of player-coach if that would help me make the club.

As it turned out, I did enough to earn a spot with the Marlins, making them the third different Torborg-managed team that I played for. That has to be some kind of record. The players on Florida's young roster liked to kid me about taking Geritol and needing a walker. I took the jokes in stride, responding that my "Dominican age" was 33, a reference to the uncertain ages of some players who come from certain parts of Latin America. I probably would have burned out in my midthirties if I didn't have the ability to laugh at myself.

I started only a handful of games during the 2002 season, never really finding my rhythm at the plate, but I enjoyed every minute of what I knew would be my last season. The Marlins had a talented group of young players who were just a year away from putting it all together and winning a championship.

I returned to Montreal for the final time during the last week of the season. My former team, which had already inducted me into its hall of fame, honored me during a pregame ceremony. I took the field for my 2,500th career game and proceeded to commit an error and hit into a double play, another sign that Father Time had caught up to me. With speculation still swirling about the future of baseball in Montreal, I hoped that my last game in the city wouldn't be *the* last game in the city. (It wasn't. The Expos remained on life support for two more seasons before relocating to Washington for the 2005 season.)

Before the last game of the 2002 season, I officially announced my retirement, making it clear that this time there was no coming back. "It's been a great ride," I said at a press conference. Torborg gave me a rare start in the season finale against the Philadelphia Phillies. I went 1-for-3 before quietly leaving the game before the start of the sixth inning. Afterward, I showered, got changed, and cleaned out my locker for the last time.

I wanted to take some time off to relax and be with my family, who had sacrificed a lot so that I could enjoy a long and fruitful career. They knew how much I loved the game, and I wanted to make sure I took some time to show how much I loved them.

A person with as much baseball in his blood as I do can't stay away from the game for very long. I became a roving instructor in the Marlins system before accepting an offer to manage the Brevard County Manatees, the Expos' Florida State League team, for the 2004 season. Those jobs didn't take me too far from home and allowed me to balance baseball and family life.

In my first and only season managing in the FSL, I was in good company, because Hall of Famer Mike Schmidt was also making his debut as the skipper of the Philadelphia Phillies' team in Clearwater. Both Mike and I had to get used to a minor league lifestyle neither of us had experienced in decades. That meant carrying my own bags and staying in cheap motels, but it also gave me an opportunity to mentor young players without the pressure of worrying about my own performance.

I enjoyed working with the players but was less enthusiastic about all of the paperwork that the job required, including daily reports to the Expos front office about every player and the progress of the team. I was a hit-and-run guy, not a pencil-and-pen guy, a reality that made my stay in Brevard County brief. The Manatees went 53–72 in my only season at the helm, but I took satisfaction in beating the best team in the league, the Vero Beach Dodgers, more often than they beat us. As a manager in the Expos system, I had the privilege of sitting on the bench for the Expos' swan song in Montreal.

With a couple of notable exceptions, I didn't look back on my life in baseball with many regrets. Obviously, I would have loved to win a championship in Montreal, and the failure to do so qualifies as the greatest disappointment of my career. The Expos' move to Washington guaranteed for the time being that no one would ever experience the thrill of bringing a World Series title to Montreal. That might change some day, but I'm not holding my breath. Baseball commissioner Rob Manfred acknowledged in 2016 that he was open to the possibility of bringing baseball back to Montreal, but a lot of pieces would need to fall into place for that to happen.

I only played five seasons with the White Sox, but I grew close enough to the city and organization during that time to feel a vested interest in bringing a championship to the South Side of Chicago. That's why I jumped at the opportunity to join White Sox manager Ozzie Guillen's coaching staff for the 2005 season. Adding to the appeal of the job was that Ozzie and general manager Ken Williams hired a number of other former players to the coaching staff, including the legendary Harold Baines and my former teammate and ping pong whiz Joey Cora.

The White Sox, who were coming off their third straight second-place finish in the American League Central, brought me in to coach first base and work with players on base running. The 2005 team looked to be really good, with Paul Konerko and Jermaine Dye leading an offense that set a club record for home runs a season earlier. Mark Buehrle, Freddy Garcia, and Jon Garland anchored the pitching staff. I enjoyed working with Japanese import Tadahito Iguchi and Scott Podsednik, who the White Sox acquired to add speed to their power game. It worked. Podsednik, who led the National League in stolen bases in 2004, swiped 59 bags in '05. Iguchi had 15 steals, and Aaron Rowand added 16.

The combination of power, speed, and pitching took the White Sox to new places, and it was a joy to be along for the ride. After winning 99 games and the division title, we ripped through the competition in the postseason, losing only one game, in the American League Championship Series, en route to the White Sox's first title since 1917. I'm not sure that winning a World Series as a coach is the same as winning one as a participant, but as someone who had two rings as a player, I found special meaning in getting another as a coach. I was equally excited for my onetime teammate Frank Thomas, who, after 16 years with the White Sox, finally got to play on a championship team in his last season in Chicago. Unfortunately, Frank didn't participate in the postseason due to injury, but he got a tremendous ovation when he threw out the first pitch of Game 1 of the ALDS.

I came back the following season as a bench coach for the White Sox but didn't last long in that capacity. After the 2006 season, in which we finished in third place with 90 wins, the White Sox chose not to renew my contract. I had seen managers and their assistants come and go dozens of times during my playing career, but experiencing it firsthand hammered home the fact that major league coaching jobs offer very little stability. To this day I can't figure out why I was the only coach let go. Guillen and I had a pretty good relationship, but maybe the chemistry between us just wasn't there. I didn't feel bitter about it. Some say Ozzie resented my sense of humor and wanted to be the only one providing comic relief in the clubhouse. That's a strange reason not to want to work with someone, but at the end of the day, it was the White Sox, not Ozzie, who fired me.

As I weighed my options, I thought again about Tim Jr., who I had played against and with. That left one last scenario. I was his father, so it made sense that he would play *for* me. As I packed up my things in Chicago, I added that to my "to do" list.

I eventually landed a managerial job with the Newark Bears of the independent Atlantic League. Because the Bears weren't affiliated with a major league team, I wouldn't be called on to file any lengthy reports to the main office. If a team had interest in one of my players, it would have to pick up the phone and call me or send a scout down.

From the get-go, I really enjoyed the experience. A lot of the guys who played for me were former big-leaguers looking to earn another shot in the majors. One of them, Carl Everett, had been shadowing me ever since my retirement. In 2004, he came to Brevard County on a rehab assignment with the Expos. The next season, we both went to the White Sox organization. And in 2009 and 2010, he played for me in Newark. Carl stirred up a lot of controversy during his career. His attention-grabbing actions ranged from telling reporters that dinosaurs never existed to getting into physical or verbal altercations with umpires and fans. He definitely marched to the beat of his own drummer. In my first year in Newark, Carl was the best player on my team, hitting .315 with 17 home runs and 82 RBIs.

About half the players I managed in Newark in 2009 had previous major league experience. That group included Pete Rose Jr. and my son, who hadn't played a major league game since 2004. Tim Jr. played four games for me before signing a minor league deal with the Kansas City Royals. He never made it back to the big leagues, retiring in 2011 with a .213 average in 160 at-bats and 10 stolen bases in 13 attempts. His minor league numbers were much more impressive: in 12 seasons, he accumulated over 1,200 hits and more than 450 stolen bases.

Little Rock didn't have the kind of career I did, obviously, but I'm extremely proud of him for reaching the highest level of the sport. That's an accomplishment that very few people can claim. In what turned out to be his last season of professional ball, he came back to play for me in Newark, hitting .294 with 20 stolen bases.

CHAPTER THIRTEEN

13

TIM RAINES, HALL OF FAMER. It's a distinction I never dreamed possible. For much of my childhood, I envisioned myself going professional in football, not baseball. But baseball became my calling.

I didn't play the game for individual accolades. I finished second to Fernando Valenzuela in Rookie of the Year voting and never won a Gold Glove or MVP award. The greatest accomplishment of my career was playing on two World Series–winning teams in New York. But when all was said and done, I had racked up some pretty impressive statistics.

In 2008, I became eligible for induction into the Hall of Fame, receiving 24 percent of the vote, not a bad total for a first-timer on the ballot. Rich "Goose" Gossage was the only person who received enough support to make it to Cooperstown that year. Three others on that ballot—Jim Rice, Andre Dawson, and Bert Blyleven— eventually surpassed the 75 percent threshold needed to get in.

I wasn't expected to get to Cooperstown in my first year of eligibility. Not a whole lot of players make it in on the first ballot, meaning a lot of other guys who had great careers have to remain patient. That wasn't too difficult for me. When I started out in the game, I didn't know whether I had what it took to stay a major-leaguer for very long. And even after I experienced unimaginable success, I still never thought of myself as being in the same class as the all-time greats.

But, truth be told, I warmed to the idea over time. My love affair with the game was so strong that I started daydreaming about what it would be like to join the ranks of players I idolized or played with and against.

It seemed like some voters weren't sure how to handle a guy who openly battled cocaine addiction early in his career. Jim Fanning, my former Expos manager, referred to it as "the drug thing," telling reporters that I'd be a shoo-in for the Hall of Fame otherwise. I never felt the need to campaign for induction. That's just not my style. But I was fortunate to have a lot of supporters openly supporting my candidacy. Jonah Keri, a writer for *Sports Illustrated* who also authored an excellent book about the history of the Expos and wrote the introduction to the one you're reading, became one of my most vocal and passionate advocates. Jonah and a lot of people made the case for me better than I could have made it for myself, citing new sabermetric statistics that have gained a lot of popularity in recent years. According to the "wins above replacement" stat, which basically tells you how many games a team won based on an individual player's performance, I rank as the sixth-best left fielder of all time, behind Barry Bonds, Ted Williams, Rickey Henderson, Carl Yastrzemski, and Manny Ramirez. That's pretty good company.

A few years after my drug problem became public, the sports edition of the board game Trivial Pursuit included the following question: What Montreal Expos speedster admitted using $40,000 worth of cocaine in the first nine months of 1982? Anybody who answered "Tim Raines" got a pie piece. Now, 35 years later, I hope the makers of the game will revisit that question. I'm thinking something along the lines of, "What former Montreal Expos speedster overcame drug addiction and went on to enjoy a 23-year major league career that culminated with his induction into the Baseball Hall of Fame?"

It's funny how quickly a career unfolds. I woke up one day as a member of the Chicago White Sox and realized I had become an elder statesman. And that extended to all aspects of the game. It had been 10 years since I beat my cocaine addiction, but I looked around me and saw other players waging battles of their own with the drug. One of them was my former Expos teammate Otis Nixon, who got arrested for cocaine possession in the late 1980s and missed the 1991 World Series with the Atlanta Braves after testing positive for drugs. Otis and I had similar skill sets, meaning we both could run and hit. I remembered the support I got from Andre Dawson during my darkest hours and felt compelled to reach out to Otis to offer my support. It didn't matter that we played for different teams. He was a human being with a problem that I could relate to, and I wanted to help.

In my first years of eligibility, I didn't think too much about my chances of induction. Every January, when the votes were counted, I'd check on how many I got and then put it out of my mind for another year. I felt honored that people would even consider electing me to the Hall of Fame. As the years passed and my percentage of the vote started to climb toward the magic number of 75 percent,

I started thinking about it more, especially after the Hall of Fame decided in 2014 that players would remain on the ballot for a maximum of 10 years, not 15 as had been the case before. I actually lost votes between 2013 and 2014, so that rule change didn't bode well for me. Dawson, who had to wait nine years to reach Cooperstown, helped calm me down. "Homey, it's a process," he'd tell me. "Don't worry about it. You're going to get in."

In 2015, my vote total started climbing again. Sensing that things were starting to break my way, Hawk told me to fasten my seatbelt and enjoy the ride. I've never known him to be wrong about anything, and I hoped this wouldn't be the first time.

It wasn't. In 2017, I got the call.

Entry into the Hall of Fame is the culmination of a life's work. My journey to Cooperstown started when I picked up a bat and glove for the first time when I was five years old and continued in ways I never dreamed of. My dad, who worked his butt off for 50 years working construction, helped nurture my skills so that I would have opportunities he never did. That's why I consider induction into the Hall a group accomplishment. Without my family and friends and teammates, I never would have come close to enshrinement.

Life moves pretty quickly, and I feel blessed to have spent so many of my days on a baseball field.

Ballplayers have lives like everyone else, though. My first marriage ended in 2005, and a couple of years later I met and eventually married my wife, Shannon, who is from Ottawa. In September 2010, Shannon and I had twin girls, Amelie and Ava. My new life has been awesome in every sense. My daughters keep me on my toes with their energy and enthusiasm. They have no idea how fast their dad used to be. Since having hip surgery a couple of years ago, I've lost another step or two. When we play tag on the playground, they catch me more often than any catcher did during my major league career.

On the day of the announcement in January 2017, I woke up early and shot hoops with my daughters before helping them get ready for school. In the weeks leading up to the results of the vote, I tried my best to explain to them what it meant to be elected to the Hall of Fame. That was tougher than it sounds. I showed them old footage of me playing the game, which they got a kick out of. "Is that you, Daddy?" they asked suspiciously. I guess the young guy running around the bases in those videos doesn't look a whole lot like the old guy they know as their dad. Despite not seeing the resemblance, Amelie and Ava assured me that I would still get their Hall of Fame vote, if they had one.

My wife and daughters were sitting by my side at our Phoenix-area home when I got the call from the Hall of Fame. Jack O'Connell of the Baseball Writers Association of America phoned with the news that I received 86 percent of the vote. "I don't know what it is with the Montreal people, but you guys seem to have to wait longer than everyone else," he joked. Soon after, I learned that Jeff Bagwell and Ivan "Pudge" Rodriguez had also gained entry to the Hall.

My parents were the first to find out about my induction. I had already let them know that early voting returns indicated I had an excellent chance of getting in and that I'd call them as soon as I received the news. Once it became official, I phoned them as soon as I could. My mom picked up on the first ring. "I'm in," I told her and my dad, who had picked up another line. They let out a yelp of excitement that almost brought tears to my eyes.

I had to hold it together, though, because the festivities were just beginning. After taking the Hall of Fame call in private, I did a conference call with some sportswriters and then sat for several on-camera interviews. I had enough time to enjoy a barbecue dinner with my family before my agent, Randy Grossman, and I boarded a red-eye flight bound for New York, where I attended a press conference and other events. I didn't sleep a wink on the plane and had to rely on adrenaline getting me through the rest of the week and weekend.

In the whirlwind days that followed, my life flashed before my eyes as I accepted congratulations from so many of the people whose love, friendship, and support helped pave the way for my success. I got calls from people I hadn't spoken to in years, including former Montreal Expos owner Charles Bronfman and my former high school baseball coach, Bobby Lundquist. Both were overjoyed at the news of my induction. Bronfman promised me that busloads of Montrealers would come to Cooperstown for the induction ceremony. Justin Trudeau, the Canadian prime minister, weighed in with congratulations on Twitter. I also got a call from the great Joe Morgan. It took several weeks to return all of the hundreds of phone and text messages that streamed in.

In New York, I shared some nice moments with Jeff Idelson and Jane Forbes Clark of the Hall of Fame, as well as with Bagwell and Rodriguez, neither of whom I knew very well. As a base runner, I had stood next to Bagwell at first base a few times in the early 2000s, but we didn't say much, if anything, to each other. Pudge said he had tried to tell me something from behind the plate when he caught a game against the White Sox in the early 1990s but that I hadn't listened…probably because he was speaking in Spanish. "I said, 'Don't even think of trying to steal against me,'" Pudge recalled telling me. "Then you stole third." Now that we would be forever linked in baseball history, I figured it was a good time to develop more of a relationship with Bagwell and Pudge. We hit it off well in New York.

Slowly, the numbness I felt upon receiving the news of my induction started to wear off. I could then reflect a little better on what it all means. Election to the Hall of Fame completed the journey of a small-town boy whose life in baseball's fast lane brought him early success, much-needed redemption, and ultimate joy. I became only the fifth player in baseball history to earn entry to the Hall in his last year of eligibility, but it was absolutely worth the wait.

I'll leave you with this final thought: I appreciated every moment I spent in a baseball uniform, and it's gratifying to know that so many people appreciated what I accomplished. A career is made up of thousands of little moments and pieces. When we look back on our careers, all we can hope is that we've created a body of work that we can be proud of. I reflect on my career with tremendous pride. Being told that my body of work makes me among the best to ever play the game is just a bonus.

Acknowledgments

THIS BOOK WOULDN'T HAVE BEEN possible without the support of so many people who have touched my life.

Charles Bronfman, John McHale, Dick Williams, Jim Fanning, and others in the Expos organization helped me to become a man and contributed greatly to my triumphs in Montreal.

During my 23 years in the majors, I formed a lot of friendships that have stood the test of time. Writing this book gave me a chance to reflect on those special relationships. Andre Dawson was always there for me in Montreal, and when I asked him to write the foreword to this book, he was there for me again.

I feel fortunate to have shared a field and clubhouse with a lot of class acts in Chicago and New York. For obvious reasons, the championship years with Joe Torre and the Yankees remain among my most cherished.

The process of writing this book took me back in time to when I was a kid in Sanford, Florida, trying to excel at every sport I played. I owe a debt of gratitude to all of my coaches at the youth level and Seminole High School for helping to nurture my talents.

Throughout my career, I drew inspiration from guys who played the game the way I did. Lou Brock, Rickey Henderson, and Vince

Coleman were kindred spirits. And Joe Morgan, George Brett, Dave Winfield, and Hal McRae were role models.

My agent and friend, Randy Grossman, has stood by my side for many years and provided invaluable help in putting this book together. Before Randy, there were Tom Reich and Adam Katz, both outstanding agents.

Thank you to Tom Bast, Adam Motin, and the publishing team at Triumph Books for giving me the opportunity to tell my story.

I am so thankful to have such a wonderful family. My parents, Ned Sr. and Florence, raised me right and have been my biggest fans over the years. My wife, Shannon, and our girls, Ava and Amelie, inspire me every day. And I'm proud of the men that my sons, Tim Jr. and Andre, have become.

Thanks to Jonah Keri for his introduction to this book and for his advocacy. Jonah, Ryan Spaeder, and Matthew Ross took it upon themselves to tell voters why they thought I deserved to be in the Hall of Fame.

Finally, thanks to the fans, especially those in Montreal, who hopefully someday will have another team to root for.

—Tim Raines

FIRST AND FOREMOST, I WOULD like to thank Tim for the opportunity to help tell his story. Long before Cooperstown called, Tim was a member of the Nice Guys Hall of Fame.

As always, the team at Triumph Books helped make the entire process smooth.

Thanks to Andre Dawson, Warren Cromartie, Steve Rogers, Jim Wohlford, David Palmer, Frank Thomas, and Bernie Williams for sharing their memories of playing with Tim. And thanks to Ned and Florence Raines for filling in some details about Tim's childhood.

Thanks to Scott Crawford from the Canadian Baseball Hall of Fame, and to unofficial Expos historian Russ Hansen, who offered invaluable guidance and support throughout the project.

Thanks to Steve Fortunato for his help and to Randy Grossman for all of his hard work and input.

Thanks, finally, to my parents and sister for their support and to my wife and daughters for everything they give me.

—Alan Maimon